nily goes beyond blood · We can surmount

at discoveries · We all have a uniq

netimes it's what you don't ask for that is th

yond blood · Photos capture mem

net just might appear · The grass is greener on the other side of the fence...So? · Love

trange · You can't always go it alone · It pays to approach new things

h an open mind · The most meaningful legacies can't be measured · It's good to be in

nerica · Family history is worth hanging onto · Age is just a number ·

nning matters...sometimes · The best things to own are those you earn · Meaningful

nore beautiful · Friendship is hard, but the rewards are grand

u might be more like your parents than you'd like to admit · Work can be sacred ·

's up to you how colorful your life is · Just sitting can be pure joy

en the wounded have the capacity to heal others · Perfection is overrated · It's not the

e of the gift that counts · Love is bigger than squabbles · Love can

dure across continents · You can be anything you imagine · The world is filled with

nder · Take time to stop and taste the chocolate · You never

ow what is hidden inside · Sometimes the cynics are just plain wrong · Letters are bet-

· We can surmount tragedy with love · The best way to cross the

ish line is one step at a time · Letters are better · You can live richly, and money has

thing to do with it · You can handle more than you think · We

n surmount tragedy with love · Kindness is a language the whole world speaks ·

titude is half the battle · Work can wait · On your to-do list, it's a good idea

put people first · You can't fail unless you stop trying · Pets are part of the family ·

ometimes you've got to think outside the box · Even small

ps are important · Pets are part of the family · It's never too late to be what you might

ve been · True surprise is a rare gift · It's wonderful to be human · Your

ntribution is more valuable than you might think · Objects are just objects...what

a gift for:

---

from:

50 truths *worth* knowing

BOK 4126

Visit us on the Web at www.Hallmark.com.

Cover Photo by Hallmark Cards, Inc.

Interior Photos are © by Hallmark Cards Inc., Getty Images (Botanica, Brand X Pictures, Hulton Archive, Image Bank, Image Source, Photo Alto, Photodisc, Photographer's Choice, Reportage, Stockbyte, Tony Stone), Christine Taylor, Corbis, Photonica, Superstock, Taxi and Veer.

Printed and bound in China

ISBN: 1-59530-103-8

First Edition, June 2005

19 18 17 16 15 14 13 12 11 10

50 truths *worth* knowing

contents

Leeds
Hull
Manchester
Norwich
Birmingham
ENGLAND
London
Bristol
Dover
Calais
Boulogne
Southampton
Plymouth
CHANNEL
Le Havre
Paris
Dijon

ONE

love can endure across continents

We had dated barely a year, but I knew in my soul that she was the one for me. A simple, random harmony that just wouldn't quit: the drape of raven hair, her wicked, jolting sarcasm, and something about that gentle indentation in her upper lip. All conspired to make me thoroughly hers. How could I spend an entire summer without her?

Laura had fallen for me, too, but here was a chance for her to see the far side of the world on a Fulbright teaching scholarship. She would travel through India for nearly three months, visiting holy shrines, meeting cultural leaders, and storing it all away to share with her world history students back home. Of course I urged her on, thrilled at her opportunity, and only half joked that even though we would be in separate hemispheres, our souls would be joined every moment we were apart. "Namaste," we would laugh, invoking the Sanskrit word used by Hindus across the Indian subcontinent to communicate reverence, honor, togetherness.

She boarded her plane in a roiling summer thunderstorm, the flashes of lightning seeming to sear each of our good-byes into our souls. I drove home alone, wondering how our time apart might pull at the delicate threads we'd woven between us. Would being apart help us to love each other more? Then later that night, as the thunder and rain began to ebb, I found a trove of greeting cards Laura had left for me. She had written nearly a dozen, each earmarked for a week she would be gone, and I read them one by one as the summer wore on, parceling out a steady diet of her happy, reassuring words.

On my side of the planet, I composed long typewritten letters and faxed them to the exotic dialing codes listed on Laura's travel itinerary, timing each one to arrive just as she checked into hotels in Delhi, Madras, Calcutta, and other parts of India. Finally, near her journey's end, I set up a makeshift recording studio at my kitchen table and filled a cassette tape with bits of her favorite music, poetry, and stories, along with news of her family and friends. Laura would later recall the most sublime moment of her trip: sitting on the hotel balcony in the sweltering

Indian summer after a monsoon rain, listening to the sound of my voice float across the courtyard as wild monkeys frolicked and chattered in the dripping palm trees.

And then what seemed an eternity finally ended. Laura's plane was headed home. I stood at the end of the long airport concourse, surrounded by taxi and limousine drivers waiting for their inbound passengers. As the travelers cleared customs, the drivers held up handwritten signs to beckon their rides—"Robert," "Citicorp," "IBM," "Mr. Singh." Then the woman I'd fallen for, missed all summer, and a year later would marry burst through the gate to run toward me.

I held up my own sign, etched with the single word that said everything I held in my heart: I bow to you. There is no other. We are joined always. "Namaste."

BY TONY FARRELL

TWO

the best way to cross the finish line is one step at a time

When we were in high school, my brother, coming off a season of cross-country racing, impulsively decided he'd run a marathon. I was jealous and privately resolved that I'd someday run a marathon, too. But there was college, then grad school, then work, and before I knew it, I had two children and was contemplating my 40th birthday.

Through it all, I kept running, but never seriously and never with a training program. If I decided I wanted to enter a 5K or a 10K, I just ran a little more than usual. The marathon dream kept getting pushed back…maybe when the kids were teenagers. That was only 11 years away, after all.

But one day, sitting at work, I received an E-mail from a fit friend: "Have you ever considered running a marathon?" Only for the past 26 years! It was just a few weeks earlier that I'd finished a half-marathon feeling good, almost good enough to keep on going. Now, with my friend's involvement, I'd have a support system. I decided to try it.

So I chose a spring event—Virginia Beach's Shamrock Marathon. I found a beginner's training plan online, tacked it to the wall, and never looked back. I did whatever the plan told me to do. Three miles, nine miles, 18 miles, rest days. If bitterly cold weather forced me to the dreaded treadmill, I climbed on. If 4 inches of snow had fallen the day before, I sloshed through it. I learned to leave my family for Sunday runs. Sometimes after a multi-hour run, I'd find myself lugging my 25-pound toddler son around, but I wrote it off as strength training. The goal eliminated all barriers. I believed that if I did each day's training, the 26.2 miles would be a breeze. And it almost was.

But after all the miles I'd racked up, I forgot to arrange for a decent 5 a.m. breakfast on marathon day, a lapse that caught up with me in the final 5 miles. I fought the fatigue, the wind, and increasing self-doubt by remembering how I'd taken the training one day at a time—making time for the runs, learning to pace myself through the miles, and focusing on each step of training as part of the larger goal. I kept thinking about how far I'd come and that just a few more steps would get me to the finish. And I got there, finishing in just under four hours, reaching my goals (*one, to finish; two, to finish in the 4-hour range*), but completely depleted.

I got the flyer for next year's marathon in the mail yesterday. Will I do it? I haven't decided yet. But I know I can.

BY CHRISTINE BUCHER

work can wait

Even before I took the job, I knew it would be a risk. After all, the statistics on start-ups aren't good. But the payoff—a good career move and a bigger salary—was too good to pass up. So I quit my old job. My wife and I relocated, 6-month-old child in tow. We bought a house. Jen stayed home with our son—an arrangement that we'd both wanted from the time Gabe was born and that the new job allowed us to afford—and I worked.

In fact, I did little else but work. Long days in the office, nights at home, and plenty of weekends were absorbed by the machinations of the corporate world as I managed people and projects and tried to keep the whole endeavor on track.

Then, on the very day of my one-year anniversary on

the job, the owner walked in, said that we'd had our successes, but he was pulling his funding. We were done. Two days later, the offices were empty, and I was home.

The next few days, or weeks, were a jumble of confused emotions. Jen and I pulled our finances together, talked about job options, and tried to make sense of what had happened without dwelling on the harsh reality of what we could be facing. But I was no longer completely consumed with work. In between the phone calls and conversations about future prospects, I spent time with my son. Instead of leaving for work while Gabe ate breakfast and coming home when he was already asleep and hearing about his antics from my wife, I witnessed his life, firsthand. I watched him walk—everywhere. No more crawling. He liked to feel the bark on the elm trees in the backyard. He chased the dog. He could say "mommy." And "daddy." And he smiled when he said it. He'd take my hand, lead me across the room, and have me sit down with him to build something with his blocks that he could demolish or to play with his trucks or to read him a book. It was that little hand, reaching out for mine, that made me realize what I had sacrificed over the previous year.

It's what too many fathers give up in the climb to the top: time with family. Careers and businesses are built while the kids stay home with mom or go to day care. It isn't that it's wrong; most of the time it's a necessity. But it creates a small crack in the father/child relationship. Shortly after my job evaporated, I started taking Gabe to a group playtime in town so that he could be around other kids. I was the only father there. And when other dads would occasionally show up, they stuck out like sore thumbs. Not because they were men, but because they seemed so unsure of what they were doing. So uncomfortable. That kind of close interaction is simply foreign to most dads. They honestly don't know what to do, because they've never had the opportunity to learn. Work has eaten away the time.

Eventually, I'll be back in an office, pouring time and attention into a new project, dedicating myself to its success. But not yet. I'm making plans for play group. Some things are just more important than work.

BY BRIAN FISKE

BY AIR MAIL
PAR AVION

FOUR

letters are better

In a wooden frame hung in the stairwell of my parents' home is a black-and-white photograph of my grandmother as a nurse during World War II. She's sitting on the stairs leading up to a tiny wooden building with a bright, playful grin on her face. No doubt she's either flirting with the cameraman or dreaming wistfully of a boy fighting overseas. But it's the papers, yellowed with age and tucked in the frame beside the photograph, that truly touch my heart. It's a letter from her father, one of the last she would receive before his death, saved in a box for more than 50 years until she, too, passed away.

Letters, perhaps the most personal type of long-distance communication, are now all but obsolete. Good writing skills and elegant penmanship were once critical to sharing small-town news with relatives across the country or confessing enamored thoughts and affections to a lover miles away. The hours once spent obsessing over just the right words to express deeply felt emotions have since been replaced by a hastily typed "I luv u" or, worse yet, a kissing smiley face formed with typographical symbols :-*. Friends across the globe can send messages and even hold conversation in a matter of seconds through high-speed cable lines. And for particularly personal conversations, you can interrupt almost anyone's life 24 hours a day, 7 days a week, through a small ringing device attached to their hips (*also known as a cellular phone*). But somehow, this isn't quite the same.

There's still something special about mail. The real thing. That hand-addressed envelope calling out to you from between all those bills and mail-order catalogs. Letters you can hold and fold and words you can read and reread until your heart's content, communication that yellows with time yet finds a special place in a secret drawer or box of memoirs—instead of piling up in an electronic in-box that you always forget to print out.

It's the thought that so obviously went into each sentence, each word, each letter formed. It's finding the envelope, the address, the stamp. These things all take time, a precious commodity that so many of us lack these days.

But it's in the giving of our time, the seconds and minutes we cherish so deeply, that allows others to see how much we care.

It's why my grandmother kept that letter from her father. Fifty years later, it was still a reminder of his love.

BY KATIE CHAFIN

you never know what is hidden inside

The moment had come for the students in my creative arts class to choose their animal assignments. And Anthony was worried.

Ever since a professional symphony had invited our class to accompany their performance of Saint-Saen's "Carnival of the Animals" with original poetry and dance, Anthony had set his mind on being the elephant. After all, he reasoned, elephants are strong and mighty. They rule the animal world—and Anthony certainly wanted to rule third grade. But the parts for the performance would be chosen randomly from a hat.

He tried to make deals and bribe his fellow third-graders into giving him the part—to no avail. When we had a class discussion about the equal value of all animals, Anthony agreed in theory. But as sweet, quiet Esperanza stepped up to the hat, reached in, and chose the elephant, Anthony let out a moan and theatrically fell out of his chair.

Now it was his turn. As Anthony dragged himself to the hat, he rubbed his hands together and coaxed, "Come on, lion." If he couldn't have the elephant, at least he could choose something fast or strong. But when he read his pick, I knew the challenge for him and me had just increased exponentially.

Anthony was the swan. He couldn't imagine an animal less mighty. Swans are gentle and elegant. Swans don't rule anything. How could he possibly be a swan? He was crushed.

Once he recovered from the letdown, I knew deep down he could be a magnificent swan. But the recovery would have to come first, and I wasn't quite sure how to help him.

The next day I showed him a video of "Swan Lake," and we watched how the dancers moved with strength and ease. He saw the dancers jump high, like basketball players, and spin around several times without stopping. He thought maybe he could move like that. Maybe the swan wasn't so bad after all. Maybe.

So I cajoled Anthony to practice jumping and twirling. He started to get into the spirit, adding a cartwheel to his choreography. He ran and leaped and flew through the air. Elephants couldn't do that, I told him. Swans have something special that even elephants don't have. Swans have grace.

Anthony always knew he could be strong and forceful, but suddenly he had discovered that he also had ease and grace. By the time the class performed with the symphony, Anthony had become the swan. And Esperanza, usually shy, had discovered her elephant power.

BY LARA NAUGHTON

the grass is greener on the other side of the fence...so?

All the houses on my street have beautiful green lawns, and all their grass is greener than mine. Down at Steve's, a top-of-the-line sprinkler arcs back and forth nearly round the clock, keeping the soil moist, the yard cool and lush. Next door, I always see Brian laying down heaps of new seed every fall. And leave it to Rick across the street to outdo all of us each spring. He's a professional landscaper with enough know-how to push every shrub, tree, and blade of grass to its peak.

Me, I love to get out and cut, dig, rake, plant, and seed. I've nursed my lawn along with gas-powered aerators, calibrated fertilizer spreaders, self-propelled mulching lawn mowers, and electric fish-line brush whackers. I've even stretched out on the ground and pulled up the most stubborn weeds by hand. In my dirtiest, sweatiest moments, I am reduced to frontier simplicity: A man must work the land he's been given, I'll say solemnly to myself, even if it's only a quarter acre of suburban patch.

But these days, my yard is slouching—the grass competing with chickweed and clover, its green luster gone pale. This is what can happen when you become a dad.

Lucy is four years old, Will is about to turn two, and all the time I used to spend caring for my grass now goes into caring for two toddlers. Once upon a time, I'd spend an entire solitary morning raking autumn leaves into tidy piles. Now we all rake leaves together, just to make a huge pile to jump in. Before Lucy and Will, the afternoon air would be filled with the buzz and chop of hedge trimmers making perfect curves and angles of my bushes. Today, the bushes have grown long and fuzzy, and instead you'll likely hear a child sounding out the chugga, chugga, chugga of "the little engine that could" on the front step. Next week, I know I should mow at a transverse angle to maintain my fescue's sturdy health. But I'm sure I'll just roar back and forth past the front door again and again, waving as I go, and making the children scream with delight as they press their noses against the glass.

Sure, sometimes I miss working the land like I used to. But back then, the land was all I had. Now, on the lawn of my dreams, a whole family throws leaves, digs dirt, and makes the lonely sprinkler the ringleader in a circus of drenched, frolicking kids. Next door, down the way, and across the street, the grass always looks greener. But my yard has never looked better.

BY TONY FARRELL

SEVEN

7

friendship is hard, but the rewards are grand

When I moved from Portland, Oregon, back to my hometown of Philadelphia, my best friend, Rachael, was too angry to help me pack. Instead, she sulked on the dining room floor while I chipped two years' worth of ice from the freezer and jammed books into boxes.

We'd been friends and housemates for nearly seven years—two dark-haired east coast expatriates in the laid-back land of the Pacific Northwest. Rachael and I had imagined being present at the births of one another's children and growing old in the same zip code. My move back to Philadelphia stung her like a betrayal of all we'd done and dreamed.

I insisted that the move would not rupture our connection. By then, at age 30, I'd already amassed a network of far-flung friends. There was Evie, my childhood playmate, now living in Israel with her family. Judith had returned to Paris after college; Eric's tour in the Foreign Service took him to Honduras and, later, to Thailand.

I kept in touch with all of them: blue airmail pages with writing crammed between the gummed borders, postcards with richly colored stamps. I sent my friends gifts of stationery, bookmarks, chocolate chip cookies swaddled in layers of bubble wrap. Gradually, we grew accustomed to the shifting tides of long-distance friendship—several months' silence punctuated by the delight of familiar handwriting in the mailbox or an unexpected phone call on a Sunday afternoon.

But Rachael and I had never put our bond to a test of distance; we'd never lived further than ten blocks apart. Our friendship had flowered spontaneously during supermarket trips, late-night toothbrushing and gossip sessions, errands to buy lightbulbs, the daily accretion of ordinary moments.

"Let's have a phone date once a month," I proposed. "We'll take turns calling. And we'll write to each other four times a year." Rachael nodded unconvincingly.

Our first phone calls were stilted. Sharing mundane details of our days—"then I took the cats to the vet and got stuck in traffic"—seemed a waste of the long-distance dime, and conversations about The Meaning of Life felt contrived. We called less and less often; months yawned between our letters and cards.

Finally, on a visit back to Portland, we sat down for a beer in one of our old haunts. "I miss you," I said, and my eyes stung with tears.

"I miss you, too. I miss living in the same city." We gripped hands and agreed to try again—without a schedule this time, but with the renewed intention to remain connected.

Now I phone when a song on the radio reminds me of Rachael and her guitar; she calls to say that she ran into one of our former housemates. We send birthday presents and pictures of our children to stick on the refrigerator door.

Sometimes, if I am awake very late on a Thursday night, I think about my long-distance friends. In Paris, Judith may be waking up to coffee and croissants. Eric, in Thailand, is at work. In Portland, Rachael has just put the kids to bed. I imagine my friends as pulses of light sprinkled across the planet, a constellation of persistence and love. I reach for the phone, dial a number, connect the dots.

BY ANNDEE HOCHMAN

ATLANTIC
OCEAN
Bermuda
GULF OF MEXICO
MEXICO
GUATEMALA
EL SALVADOR
COSTA RICA
PANAMA
COLOMBIA
VENEZUELA
HAITI
ECUADOR
PERU
Lima
BOLIVIA
SOUTH AMERICA
BRAZIL
GALAPAGOS ISLANDS
Replogle 3.3 inch
POLITICAL GLOBE
LEGEND
PACIFIC

EIGHT

kindness is a language the whole world speaks

At the start of the new millennium, a job opportunity led my family to pack up our townhouse in suburban Washington, D.C., and move to Weil im Schönbuch, a sleepy village in southwest Germany. I spent three and a half years there tackling a language that spawned such head-pounding words as *Geschwindigkeitsbegrenzung* ("speed limit"), often with humbling results—like the time I told a neighbor that I'd be "happy to eat her cats" for her while she was on vacation. But if the language was tough to swallow, it paled in comparison to the lessons I learned about what it's like to be a foreigner in a strange land.

My neighbors tutored me and my family daily, but the language they spoke fluently to us was kindness. When I heard loud banging on my living room window late at night, I knew it was just Magda, leaning over the fence to offer me a plate of homemade, still-warm apple strudel or onion pie. When Annie and Karl drove their old tractor out to their farm on the outskirts of town, they took my five-year-old daughter along and let her sit in the exciting, bumpy side seat, then showed her how to pick potatoes out of the ground. Over time, our German friends invited us to their Sunday dinners, found me job leads, and took us places when we needed a translator. After the 9/11 terrorist attacks on America, the mayor's office even sent us a heartfelt letter, in choppy English, expressing sympathy and solidarity.

With each gesture of acceptance and inclusion, I couldn't shake a pang of shame that nicked at my conscience. Back home, a fair number of families on my block had been of Indian, Asian, and other backgrounds. While we generally were "friendly," it's how we didn't treat these non-English-native neighbors that had me queasy in hindsight. Our daughter had play dates with Ashley and Olivia, but never with Aroon from across the street, who spent his rare moments outside tossing a ball to himself. With Griesch and Ashwinda, whose townhouse adjoined ours, we'd chat for a moment while coming and going, but not once did we think to invite them for dinner or a movie. I don't know if Ashwinda had any girlfriends. If she was lonely. If she noticed our next-door distance.

If our German neighbors had treated us the way we treated these folks then, I certainly wouldn't have been feeling like I was on a grand adventure, discovering the world; I'd have felt utterly lost. I hope I always remember that I have what it takes to speak volumes with anyone. Even if I can't use many words.

BY MARIA MIHALIK HIGGINS

pets are part of the family

Pets have been part of my family for as long as I can remember. In fact, I had pets even before I was born—Philomelia, the Elegant Fowl, and the two Afghan hounds, Cleo and Robespierre. These were followed by Fon-Fon the Tulip (*a poodle*), Linus T. Aquinas (*a parakeet*), and Homer Hapilus (*the first dog I was allowed to choose, a cocker/springer spaniel mix*). My brother had a succession of guinea pigs and an evil-minded parrot named Plug John. And my sister had her own cocker spaniel, but she really wanted a cat.

Our pets gave us access to unlimited physical affection. They were always up for a game. They loved us even when our clothes were dirty or we were in disgrace for some ill-timed fight. We could tell what they were thinking—their emotions were always there for the world to see—and at dinnertime, especially, there was no mistaking what was on their minds!

We also knew that they could tell what we were feeling—if we'd been hurt or humiliated at school, if we were sad or angry, if we just needed a hug. If our sister had pinched us, the dog would comfort us. If no one would talk to us, the parakeet would sing for us. Childhood is never lonely when animals are there.

It's also never boring! You never knew what any of those characters would be up to next. There was the time my pet anoles, the Borgias, Cesare, and Rodrigo, escaped from their tank. I was convinced my reptile-hating mother would evict both them and me if she found out about it. I was in despair until I saw that the little lizards were so excited by their adventure that they'd turned bright green, a dead giveaway on the brown chair leg they had chosen for their escape route. And the time my dog Hapilus had a field day eating the fermented pears that had dropped from our tree in late August—he reeled around grinning from ear to ear for a week.

Pets are a family's love made visible. They make it easy to learn to display affection, receive affection, return affection. And they are the best teachers. They teach us true family values—love for its own sake, loyalty, fidelity, friendship, trust, and playfulness. Through them, we grow to be better people, because they take us to their hearts and show us what really matters. As my dog Molly reminds me daily, a warm, dry place to sleep, a nourishing bowl of food, and unwavering love is really as good as it gets.

BY ELLEN PHILLIPS

TEN

even small steps are important

This was the dream: ten weeks of teaching, and I'd transform their lives. Twenty-eight elmentary students, mostly African-American, living in a working-class West Philadelphia neighborhood, would travel with me into the world of poetry and emerge with hearts made tender by the trip.

This was the reality: a trailer parked outside an over-crowded public school, a pebbled chalkboard, 28 kids complaining because they were having poetry instead of snacks.

Even after a decade as a visiting writer, I still brought passion to the job; on the first day, I nearly brought myself to tears reciting a poem about survival in the face of life's obstacles. I hoped the kids would identify with the message; instead, Jeffrey hunched over his paper, obsessively drawing superheroes with jagged wings. Olivia tossed her microbraids and rolled her eyes.

I offered a writing topic close to home: "Shut your eyes and imagine the block where you live…how it sounds…how it smells…how it feels."

"There ain't nothin' in my neighborhood," Abram insisted. I sat down next to him, asked questions, then wrote while he dictated: "My block is loud: I hear gun-shots and cursing…My block is the feeling of madness when people cry and they're sad."

Through a bitter winter of Tuesdays, we hunkered in the trailer and wrote: *Yellow tastes like banana pudding. Love is the feeling of almost crying.* Rashan painstakingly typed: *Sadness is when someone dying/sadness is when someone crying/sadness is when someone get buried.*

But the hooting and jumpiness never stopped; I spent more time demanding quiet than I did praising their poems. On the next-to-last day, I pleaded for order. Khadijah ducked under the table; Najmah leapt from her seat, shouting; Rashan dropped his pants.

"STOP IT!" I screamed, shocking the group into silence. I thought of those aerosol cans labeled CONTENTS UNDER PRESSURE. I had no idea what I would do next. All of us were saved by the lunch bell. The kids burst out of the trailer. I burst into tears. Poetry was too thin a medium, I thought, to bridge my life and theirs. I had no words to ease Rashan's sadness, no rhyme to soften the reality of a neighborhood that echoes with gunshots and curses.

I attended their final performance—before an audience of parents, teachers, and classmates—because I had to. One by one, my students read, while I waited anxiously for the whole event to dissolve into a nightmare of shouting and spitballs. Instead, I saw K-lam's face open into a huge smile as the audience applauded his poem. I heard Deja declare that the ocean is "a joy of salty tears." And I thought of another child, a girl who—after a week of intensive instruction on metaphors—wrote on her evaluation, "I learn to say thank you after every poem."

The lesson I aim to teach is not necessarily the one my students need to hear. But perhaps the lesson they absorb is the one I most need to remember. Say thank you after every poem. Be grateful for any tenuous step.

After they read, I whispered "thank you" to each small face, and in exchange received a poem, the paper creased from nervous hands, a scrawled but legible gift.

BY ANNDEE HOCHMAN

ELEVEN

you can't fail unless you stop trying

I was 40 years old, with a beautiful seven-year-old son and a husband I adored. But I was disgusted with myself.

I'd quit smoking when I learned that my little boy was on the way…only to start again when he was a year old. When he was five, I quit for almost a year. After that, I managed to stop for a few days or weeks here and there. But mostly, I smoked.

I lit up in the house and in the car, even at my son's soccer games under other mothers' accusing eyes. Craving nicotine, I snuck out of his birthday parties and school functions, and once stole out of a family member's funeral to smoke outside the church.

I was disgusted with myself, but I was also afraid. Emphysema, lung cancer, heart attack, stroke…they could happen to me. I smoked, quit, and started again. After each failure, I was more ashamed and frightened, and fell further into despair.

But always, a voice inside whispered that I couldn't stop trying; my son depended on me. My life was precious—I was precious. Fight, the voice whispered. So after each failed attempt, I quit again. And again.

I knew that this voice was God's and that He would not give up on me as long as I didn't give up on myself. But sometimes, that was difficult to believe.

One night, breathless from too many cigarettes, I dropped to my knees and called upon God. "Help me," I begged.

From deep inside me, His voice rang clear and strong.

"Do you love this life?" He asked.

"Yes," I answered.

"Are you willing to let me help you?"

"Yes," I said.

"Try again. Your faith will be rewarded," He said.

Peace dropped over me, thick and warm as a quilt, and I knew that I would stop smoking for the last time. And I have—one day at a time.

Of course, it hasn't been an easy road—to be accurate, it's been a 20-year battle. I've even slipped a few times. But always, I allow Him to step in and get me back on track. After all, failure is an illusion. Faith is our greatest weapon against adversity; and with faith comes persistence. When we embrace the struggle instead of giving in to it, we reaffirm that life is precious, worth fighting for.

Once I realized this, failure—and the faith that came from it—became a gift, a larger triumph.

BY JULIA VAN TINE-REICHARDT

TWELVE

it's wonderful to be human

I never liked being human…and therefore imperfect. I always wanted to do better. To do more. To do something wonderfully well. (*Or, rather, to do everything wonderfully well.*) No matter what my triumphs were, my mistakes would squawk at me like a neglected parakeet caged in a back bedroom. I visited my regrets at night, in the dark, trying to conjure elaborate ways to atone for my error (*however small*) and, in a sense, erase it. I wanted no black marks on my permanent record. And yet, that wasn't possible because, after all, I'm only human.

Then I learned that my father had advanced prostate cancer. He'd been diagnosed when I (*his only child*) was pregnant with his first grandchild. In the months that followed, as my daughter learned to smile and coo and sit up and grab his nose, my father hid his cancer from me until his pain became apparent.

I did all I could think to do. I brought him Italian ice in his favorite flavors—so often that the freezer bulged with leftovers. I brought my daughter with her sunshine smiles and loving hugs. I helped my mother "get things in order" at home, uncluttering closets and boxing old junk in a desperate attempt to feel in control of something. I laughed at my father's jokes…and pretended not to notice when he stopped having the strength to tell them anymore. And when he finally passed from this world, my mother and I were at his side, whispering memories of happy times at the beach, so that he'd know it was okay to go. That he'd done all he could…and all he'd needed to do.

None of what I did in those months saved my father's life. None of it reversed the cancer. None of it changed the course of his fate. But it did give me peace. For once, I realized that I had done all that I could…all that I needed to do. And when he died, I had no regrets. I still grieved, but there was no unfinished business. He knew I loved him. I knew he loved me. That was all that really mattered.

Now, when I make mistakes, I try to keep them in perspective. I try to learn from them, to apologize, to fix what I can, and then move on. The parakeet has stopped squawking. All it ever really wanted was to be set free.

I know that I cannot erase my mistakes. But I also know that I cannot remember my father's mistakes anymore—they have turned to dust. What is left is the memory of a wonderful father. A wonderful man. Not perfect...but perfectly wonderful and wonderfully human. And that is the best that any of us can really hope to be.

BY LAURA QUAGLIO

THIRTEEN

it's never too late to be what you might have been

I was 41 when my husband took me for a walk to tell me that he no longer loved me. We had two children, ages four and nine, and I was facing a hysterectomy.

When he left, I decided to remain in the four-room, small-town apartment that five years before was to have been a temporary stop while we shopped for a house. I continued to write a small Sunday newspaper column that took half my week to report and write, but paid only $100. I hoped the column's success would lead to opportunity. I pieced together other part-time income while I looked for a full-time paycheck.

A year of resumes, calls, lunches, and meetings brought no relief. The car blew its transmission. I dropped a box weighted with marriage memorabilia on my foot. The box survived; my foot broke. I fixed the car, but without health insurance, I let the foot go. I could walk, couldn't I?

The car, the kids, and I grew older. I cried when my daughter reported my son's anguish on the school bus. Anticipating good grades, he had opened his report card envelope. It was empty. He wailed. I'd fallen behind on the children's Catholic school tuition payments.

Perhaps you're knocking on the wrong doors, friends advised. Why not choose a more hospitable city and start over? Part of me liked the idea. I had dreamed of a Ph.D., of teaching, and writing books. The other part rationalized I didn't want to move the kids away from their father. Besides, I was 44—too old to start over.

Then one day I received a call from a nearby university. Three years earlier, they said, a professor had left a memo saying that if they were ever in a pinch, I could teach. The pinch arrived, the memo surfaced, and a week later I was standing in a classroom talking with 90 freshmen. I was awake and energized, researching lecture material ravenously. It felt like home. Three semesters later, I was still teaching part-time, but I needed a Ph.D. to make a career of it.

I'm too old at 46, I told myself. What school would let me in? I won't find the money. It'd be selfish to put my children through more financial hardship.

A friend, a wise woman in her eighties from Holland,

counseled me at her kitchen table. "There's no word in Dutch for 'selfish'," she said. "It isn't selfish to do what makes your eyes shine. You already have a pile of 'no.' Go out there and get the 'yes.'"

I leaned on her words like a crutch as I plodded through doctoral program applications. I taped words attributed to writer George Eliot (*the pseudonym for Mary Ann Evans*) to my computer monitor: "It's never too late to be what you might have been." I scheduled an interview with a professor at an Ivy League university.

A "yes" arrived a few months later—a four-year fellowship plus a stipend to pay the rent. Other yeses arrived, along with an offer from an editor to write a new Sunday column.

One afternoon during our first autumn in our new city, the children and I walked along a red brick sidewalk toward campus. The air was cool, the breeze robust enough to jostle the branches above our heads. My son ran ahead, twirling in a rain of yellow leaves while my daughter talked about the art class she enjoyed at her new school. We were still broke, but it didn't feel like misery, and the children were just an extra hour by car from their father. I had held out for a life with a dream attached, and we were moving toward joy.

BY SUSAN HAAS

FOURTEEN

objects are just objects... what matters most is what they represent

When my dad graduated from high school, he bought a class ring—something to mark a milestone in his education. I've often admired the gold ring, not so much because of how it looks—though it is gorgeous with a green stone set in the middle of his high school shield—but just because it belonged to my dad.

I would beg my dad to let me wear his ring. It didn't matter to me that it didn't fit my finger yet. I just wanted to share something with my dad. He finally gave in and agreed that when I graduated from eighth grade and entered high school, I could wear his ring. The deal: I could wear it throughout my high school journey until I graduated and earned my own. He and I have plans for me to be the first in my family to graduate from both high school and college. He saw the ring as motivation for me to stay in school, since my brother had already dropped out.

When the day of my eighth-grade graduation came and the ceremony ended, I got all types of presents, but the best came in a black wooden box. Inside was the gift I had anticipated, the high school ring my dad had worn for twenty-six years. My dad told me that he expected me to return it when I got my own ring; then I would make the same deal if I had a son down the road. A new tradition was beginning that day.

So for the next two years, I wore the ring every day. But when I joined the football team, I could not play or practice in jewelry of any kind. Most practice days, I'd leave the ring at home or ask my coach to hold it. Then one day my coach said he wouldn't hold it anymore, so I gave it to a friend who was watching practice. She gave it to another friend, and somewhere between the two of them and getting home before I remembered to ask for it back, it got lost.

Telling my dad the news was extremely hard, but surprisingly he wasn't angry. He told me the ring was not what was important. After all, he could buy another one. He just wants me to remember what it means to me—my promise to value my education. That's what can never be lost or tarnished. What's important is that I graduate from high school and go to college, and I still intend to—with or without the ring.

I will graduate from high school in two years, and when I do, I'm going to give my high school ring to my dad. And then, someday, I'll have a college ring to share with him, too.

BY MICHAEL TOOMER

FIFTEEN

love is strange

I met my husband at a book reading on Valentine's Day in 1997. He was tall and handsome in cowboy boots and curly hair. I, on the other hand, had on a sack dress and way too much lipstick.

I had written *The Book of Love* and was kissing copies to leave my lip prints beside my signature—a gimmick that left my face smeared in red like a kid with chapped lips. To write the book, I had interviewed tons of the "love experts" and read all the romance reports, trying to learn what it would take to meet and marry the man of my dreams. At 33, I had never been engaged. I had deserted my old boyfriend while in the process of writing and was becoming more disenchanted by the day. Now, like the shoemaker's children who had no shoes, I was the researcher of love who had lost heart.

Then, in he walked, smooth and cool, just when I was all ajitter about the thing I hated most—public speaking. He slipped off across the bookstore without introducing himself. I wiped lipstick from my cheek and sighed. They say love hits when you're not looking; they don't say it hits when you're looking strange.

At dinner, after the reading, a mutual friend introduced us. The sparks flew across a crowded table. Not only was Marc green-eyed and good-looking in a crisp white shirt and jeans, but he was funny, a first-rate furniture maker and a talented musician. The bad news was he had to leave early for band practice. The good news was he invited me to his music gig the next night.

The club was strewn in peanut shells. I took a seat at the bar with a friend. Marc strummed his guitar and sang with two Mexicans. He dedicated a Mexican love song, "The White Dress," to me. I blushed but was skeptical. He was so smooth and handsome that I had him figured for a heartbreaker. I was determined not to get hurt. Then his shoulder strap let loose and his guitar fell with a thunderous clang among the peanut shells. He looked as mortified and vulnerable as I felt. That's when I knew it could be real.

Seven days later we bought a house together. That's all it took, one week. We married on the front porch with

150 guests playing “Here Comes the Bride” in humming harmony on kazoos. To hear that somber traditional song played like warbling wax paper was crazy and beautiful all at once. It made me laugh and cry as I walked up the brick wedding aisle to where my new husband stood in black tails and cowboy boots. He was laughing, too. All I can say is: Love is strange. If you can accept that, you can live happily ever after. We certainly have.

BY CHRISTINE SCHULTZ

SIXTEEN

photos capture memories for eternity

One of the defining memories of my childhood was a Kodak commercial that ran on TV constantly. The sentimental lyrics were paired with a melody that haunts me to this day. The theme of the commercial was that you'd better photograph your children as they are now because, before you can turn around, they'll be grown and out the door and you'll have lost the moment. As I look through my photo albums today, I know that my parents took Kodak's message seriously. There we are, my brother, my sister, and me, our smiling or staring faces looking out across the decades from our photographic time capsules. As we grew older, the flurry of snapshots diminished, but by then, I'd taken up my own camera and continued the memory trail.

If I opened an album right now, they would all be

there: my grandfather standing by protectively as I, age seven, sat on his great black horse for the first time. My infant niece with her innocent blue eyes and halo of blonde curls—transformed by time and rebellion into a blood-red crewcut complemented by a tongue piercing. My first dog, half hidden beneath a blooming forsythia bush. The shot of me at age two in my party dress and bows, on a chair beside my birthday cake with a handful of illicit party mints and an expression of mixed guilt and defiance—it was my birthday, wasn't it?!—that my friends and family are probably all too familiar with to this day.

I love visiting my memories this way, being with my family, my childhood, and my growing up simply by looking in an album. As I look at the pictures, I remember the stories my parents told about the early ones—the little polar bear rug I used to hide under when scary visitors arrived; my father's family's regal European relatives, frozen in sepia on thick cardboard backing; the beautiful hand-colored portraits of my great-grandmother, whose hair remained black through her life, and my great-grandfather, whose hair turned white at sixteen. The Afghan hound who jumped over the dining room table when my great-aunt came for supper. My grandmother's adventures as a flapper and, later, as a teacher in a one-room schoolhouse.

But these days, when I look at my albums, I look

longest at the photos of my mother. I don't have many. Beautiful as she was, she seemed reluctant to pose for the camera. But I have one, taken the year she died, of the two of us sitting on the rock wall in my parents' front yard, facing each other. And the look of love in our eyes as we look at each other is so total I'd have thought it would melt the film.

Sure, my parents took pictures of their children, but they didn't forget to take photos of themselves and their parents as well. They knew that as they were building albums, they were also building memories.

BY ELLEN PHILLIPS

SEVENTEEN

if you jump, the net just might appear

The seed was planted during my college wanderings around Italy, Germany, and France. Hitting the highlights, my friend and I hadn't seen much beyond the well-worn path between the railway station and the cheapest youth hostel.

Then, on a particularly long train ride from Venice to Rome, I watched a spry young woman with frizzy pigtails and a well-worn T-shirt climb down from the luggage rack, stretching after her satisfying nap. We chatted, and I learned that she'd been on the road for 18 months with no plans of returning to "real" life anytime soon.

Awestruck by her total freedom, I asked, "How do you do it? How do you keep on going?"

She shrugged. "It's much easier than you think," she said. "You just get on the next train, and something always falls in your lap."

She showed me the doctored ticket that she'd milked for three weeks of free train travel. She told me about picking tomatoes in Spain and bussing tables in Greece, anything to stay on the road. When the work dried up or the place got boring, she'd head to the train station. After all, everywhere was only a train—or a boat or a plane ride from somewhere else.

I knew I wasn't one to falsify documents or sleep in luggage racks, but I envied her confidence. She just knew that around a turn of train track lay her next sun-drenched adventure. I resolved that one day I would do the same.

The seed she'd planted didn't sprout until I teetered on the edge of turning 30. Ensconced in a "real" but unrewarding job, putting money in my 401K, I was planning my wedding. My life looked good on paper, but I was miserable. I realized my only shot at contentment was, as Eleanor Roosevelt had commanded, to do the thing I thought I could not do.

So I made a decision: In six months, no matter what, I would leave to travel around the world. I talked to my fiancé and his own seed started to sprout.

As soon as we made the decision, the wind shifted in our favor. A major loan came from one family member. An offer of plane tickets from another. People dug gear out of closets, pressed guidebooks into our hands, told us of secret hideaways where we could live like royalty for pennies. The universe was rewarding us for listening to our dreams.

But even with these generous gifts, I began to realize that the net that had suddenly appeared was primarily composed of our own resolve. We would do anything to make it happen—quit our jobs, empty our savings, skip the big wedding, sell all of our possessions without a backward glance. Because it was our jump, and our choice, each sacrifice felt like a gift to ourselves.

Our rootless year quenched my wanderlust, and I returned home with a taste for something vastly more satisfying: the freedom and power of big risks. Whenever I wonder about taking another leap—a new job, a big move, a first child—I think back to that first sense of determination and total surrender. I know it's just that easy: Jump, I tell myself. You'll find a way.

BY MARISKA VAN AAL

EIGHTEEN

it's good to be in america

Last fall I went to my neighborhood church so I could participate in the Jewish Yom Kippur service. No, that's not a typographical error. And, yes, it is rather unconventional. Nevertheless, there I was in a church for the Yom Kippur service. And the rabbi was standing beneath a two-story-tall cross.

At first glance, that might seem strange. But then, I live in a strange neighborhood, a delightfully strange neighborhood; it's called America.

In fact, it felt a bit strange—sort of like the feeling you might have when you walk into the opposite sex's bathroom by mistake. But there I was, sitting in a church, because my synagogue down the street was in the middle of a renovation, and the church had been gracious enough to lend our congregation the use of its facility.

Naturally, the rabbi immediately addressed that issue, stating that it's perfectly all right for a Jew to pray in a church, as long as it's not habit-forming (*chuckle*). After all, a chair is a chair, walls are walls, and a prayer is a prayer.

As I surveyed my surroundings, my eyes fell on the booth where the sound and light technician for the church was sitting. He was concentrating on his work for the day: making sure the rabbi's microphone didn't squelch with feedback or that he wasn't standing in the dark when he should be in the spotlight. But I also noticed the smile on his face as he went about his work—he seemed amused and I might say pleased by the Jewish liturgy. He reminded me of my grandmother, who was deaf, but yet loved watching *I Love Lucy* on her little black-and-white TV.

Both he and my grandmother, though clueless about "the whats and the wherefores" going on before their eyes, knew in their heart of hearts that it was good and deserving of their time and attention.

His smile and the open arms of the church's congregation strengthened my faith in the warmth and openness of humankind. Yes, indeed, it's good to live in a neighborhood called America.

BY BARRY DENSA

NINETEEN

family history is worth hanging on to

In the top drawer of my old wooden desk, I keep a cassette tape that holds 100 years of history. On the tape, the voice of my great aunt Florence Farrell rises and falls, whispers and laughs as she tells tales of the house at 106 Fitch Street, the Syracuse, New York, home where she lived nearly all her 91 years.

By 1989, when I made the trip to Syracuse to sit down with Florence and tape-record her family memories for all time, four generations of Farrells had passed through the front door of the house on Fitch Street. Some of my relatives had been born there, back in an age when births almost always occurred at home. Others had died there, in the same bedrooms where they had turned off lights and settled into sleep nearly every night of their lives. Across an entire century, my Irish kin had held tight to one another, celebrated friendship and love, fought off failure and loss.

Florence remembered it all. My cousin Michael likes to say that Florence's iron-jawed memory was forged in a time when stories were gifts you exchanged with family you loved, neighbors you always knew, friends you carefully chose. In Florence's girlhood, there were no movies, no television, barely any radio. You entertained each other. Florence described for me the weekly meetings her mother would host for the Ladies' Christian Benevolent Association. Eighty years gone now: a quiet hour of tea and hazelnut cookies; a call of all present, dutifully recorded in an immense bound ledger; a discussion and agreement about charitable works and plans. And then, finally, all business done, a single LCBA member would rise from her burgundy chaise, draw a breath, and sing a song.

My tape recorder rolled on, drinking up Florence's unspooling memories, one by one. On the steps leading upstairs, there was Will, her older half brother, long since moved to New York to become an actor, but home now for a surprise visit and entertaining all with vaudeville song-and-dance routines. Now it's a Christmas Eve in the Depression, and Uncle Howard is bursting into the hallway, covered with snow and loaded with gifts for the grandkids—my own father among them—always the hero despite having bought everything half price in the final hours of holiday shopping. And then Florence tells me about finding Anthony Farrell, her father, my great-grandfather, cold and gone on a winter's morning in 1924. Father Harrison hurried right over when he received word. They laid Anthony out all day and all night in a casket in the parlor, each member of the family taking turns to sit with him. And to what purpose, a true Irish wake? I asked her.

"Respect," Florence told me. "Respect for the dead."

Barely a year after we sat together in that same front parlor, Florence passed away. But she had given me the gift of finding out that personal history is more than names or dates or a family tree. Finding out about your family history means listening long enough to the stories of your ancestors to hear them draw in breath and sing a song in your soul.

BY TONY FARRELL

TWENTY

winning matters... sometimes

My duties as a rookie Little League coach began when I picked up the faded, olive-green duffle bag full of bats, balls, and catcher's pads. This well-weathered bag could have been recycled from my playing days. It looked (*and smelled*) old enough. While the duffle bag might be the same, I vowed to avoid all the hard-boiled instruction I'd endured as a kid: One coach happily taught twelve-year-olds to take the bruises from intentionally leaning into a pitch to get on base. Another punished the team for each loss by making us run laps around the outfield. And then, there was the disaster of my dad's year as a coach; four-letter words flew faster than any pitch that season.

The yelling, pressure, and constant focus on winning spoiled the sport for me for many years. Now, as a coach to my own son and a dozen other nine- to twelve-year-olds, I was determined to make this baseball season fun for them while they learned some basic skills. When I met parents during the first practices, they were relieved to hear my philosophy of emphasizing learning and fun. And those first preseason practices went swimmingly—the only bruises were accidents.

Then, the first game.

We were blown out. After two innings, the other team was up by more than 10 runs. But we had fun, right? In the postgame meeting, we talked about all the positive things our players did and clapped for each other. No one ran "loser laps." That kind of fun lasted until we lost five games in a row. By then, the kids didn't want to show up for practice. Heads were hung lower and lower after each game, and the parents were considering swapping baseball season for cello lessons. When I announced the practice schedule after the fifth loss, excuses flew. It sounded like the only ones at next week's practices would be me and the old duffle bag.

"We're gonna do something different," I told them. "We're gonna win."

Without the yelling, without the punishment, I started emphasizing winning in the mix of things the team should also learn. They already knew how to lose—and were good sportsmen. It seemed only fair to let them taste the other side. It was a hard week of practice, and the kids seemed even more focused than me. They wanted it.

On game day, they were even more nervous than when they began the season. They squeaked out a win, but played solid, followed directions, and smiled, smiled, smiled. The parents were happy, too. Then, the team reeled off seven wins in a row. By the end of the streak, the players showed up early to practices, and parents volunteered to help carry and pack the equipment bag. Forget the cello lessons, the season was saved.

I coached six more years before hanging up the duffle bag, and after seeing six more teams of kids, I'll have to admit that winning does matter. But what mattered more (*especially after that first season*) was that the kids were looking forward to the next year.

BY DOUG DONALDSON

TWENTY-ONE

the best things to own are those you earn

I was fourteen years old when I decided to buy my own ten-speed bicycle. Up until then, Mom, Dad, and Santa Claus had always supplied my wheels, from my Radio Flyer tricycle to that first two-wheeler and on up to the sparkly-blue Schwinn Sting-Ray, with the white fiberfill banana seat and the gooseneck handlebars, I'd been riding since I was eleven.

But now I had my own vision of what a bike should be. Time to put aside the single-crank, wheelie-popping kids bike and graduate to the be-all, end-all of early-1970s high-tech pedaling: The Schwinn Continental.

Racing handlebars. Dual-shifting derailleurs. Hand-activated brakes for both front and rear wheels. Now this was serious cycling. In my Continental dreams, I imagined myself starting off with a short pedal trip of maybe, oh,

100 miles. Later, I'd find a scenic backcountry route across the state to test my endurance. Soon enough, I'd be charting a course across the USA, starting out from the West Coast and pedaling east, the better to take advantage of prevailing winds giving me a push from behind, just as the bicycling magazines promised they would.

But first I had to get the bike—and that meant I had to earn the money. I didn't need Mom and Dad to tell me; I knew the time had come to buy my own wheels. If I was big enough to mount a 24-inch alloy frame with no kickstand, then I was big enough to save up the dough.

So I opened a savings account—my first. At the bank, the teller gave me a small green passbook, each page clean and empty and ready for the handwritten entries of all the deposits I would make. Then, for nearly a year, I worked to save up the cash. I cut lawns in the spring and summer, raked leaves through the fall, and in between collected old soda bottles to return to the convenience store for the nickel deposit. Five dollars here, five cents there: the entries in the passbook slowly stacked up. Soon the book grew tattered and slightly curved from sitting so long in the rear pocket of my jeans.

Finally, the day came when I'd reached the magic monetary goal. I rode the old Sting-Ray up to the bank, and asked for the entire balance amount—a single $100 bill. It was more money than I'd ever seen, ever held in my hand, and I folded it carefully in half, put it in the pocket where the passbook had been, and rode home ever so slowly, worried that I might somehow lose it.

A few days later, I turned that bright green hundred into a yellow Schwinn Continental. The price, with tax, actually exceeded my savings, but Santa was kind enough to kick in the few extra bucks. The gears, the tires, the handlebars all belonged to me, and I recall now that while I rode the bike furiously for a time, its two wheels soon gave way to four, as I claimed the ultimate prize—my driver's license—two years later.

I never did ride from coast to coast, never dipped my bike tire triumphantly in the Atlantic Ocean at trip's end—though it remains a dream that still makes me smile. But I kept the Schwinn for many years, unwilling to let it go. After all, it was the first thing I'd ever bought that I'd truly earned. And it was the best money I ever spent.

BY TONY FARRELL

TWENTY-TWO

you might be more like your parents than you'd like to admit

Growing up, summer was project time. Each year there was a home-improvement endeavor that my father and I would work on together. Some were small and some were big, but it didn't matter if the project was a brick walkway or a two-story barn—it was just the two of us, working side by side. Often, he'd take two weeks off from his job so that we could work together all day, every day, for those two weeks.

It wasn't fun.

I'd spend hours nailing down a subfloor, or digging a trench, or framing a wall, only to have my dad say, "That's good, but it isn't right." He'd point out the misdriven nails that needed to be pulled out or where the trench should have been dug or why the wall I'd framed was out of square and have me start over again. I couldn't wait for those days to end.

And soon enough, they did. After-school and summer jobs—jobs that paid—kept me away from dad's annual summer projects. Then it was college. My first real job. A wedding. A career. The further I moved from those summer tasks, though, the more I realized what my father had really been trying to teach me: Take pride in whatever work you do. Take the time to do the job well. And leave things better than you found them.

Eventually, my wife and I bought a house of our own. We hadn't been in our new place for very long when my wife volunteered to mow the lawn; the grass obviously hadn't been cut in quite some time—the previous owner must have given up on it well before we moved in. "It'll be fun," Jen said. "I'll get to mow our very own lawn."

I kept unpacking the garage, which we were using as a storage area for piles of boxes full of stuff. In no time at all, Jen was back. "The front's done," she announced.

I stepped out of the garage and took a look. The next words that came out of my mouth? "That's good, but it isn't right." I couldn't believe it almost as soon as I'd said it—the voice was mine, but it was almost as though my father were the one speaking.

I'm lucky that my wife knows my family. Well.

Jen smiled. "You sound like your dad."

"Yeah," I sheepishly responded. "I know."

"It's okay," she said. "Your dad's a smart guy. And the grass is fine."

Fortunately, I realized she was right, on both points. After all, it's just the lawn. I wonder what Dad would say to that.

BY BRIAN FISKE

TWENTY-THREE

work can be sacred

I think about the exalted nature of joyful work—the soul-filling beauty of it—every time I look at my collection of Southwestern Pueblo pottery. Acorn-squash gold, chalky white, burnished black, or roof-tile red, these rounded vessels were originally shaped to hold seeds for next year's garden or spicy stews for ceremonial feasts or the life-giving water that only desert dwellers like the pots' makers truly value as the great treasure it is. Now—and since the railroads first opened the Pueblos to tourists in the 1880s—these beautiful vessels have been made for and prized by collectors like me.

As I pick up one of these pots (*technically called ollas*) and turn it in my hands, I think about all the love and work and artistry it took to create it. To make a pot, the potter first goes to the secret site where she and her family have found the best clay. She scrapes this into a container and brings it home, where she works tirelessly to "cure" it by kneading it with water, a process that can take months, so it will hold together when she shapes the pot. Then she creates clay coils, rolling the damp clay into "snakes" between her hands and coiling them, one strip on top of the next, to form the shape of the pot. As she builds the pot, she scrapes the thick coils with a piece of gourd or stone to make the walls thin and light, gradually revealing the final, often paper-thin form of the piece.

Once the shape is finished and has been sanded smooth and dried, the potter smoothes liquid clay—the "slip"—over its surface and burnishes it with a smooth stone to a high gloss. She may then take pigments made from carefully prepared local plants and minerals and create a design on the pot's surface. Like the shapes of the vessels and the source of the clay and pigments, these designs are often passed down in families for generations, and some of them originated in prehistoric times. Geometric and fantastic to our untrained eyes, to their makers the patterns that flow across the pots represent the beauty of nature—birds' wings, clouds, the skyline, moths and spiders. Once the pots have been painted, they are fired, traditionally outdoors under a mound of burning sheep-dung chips.

It takes days—sometimes weeks—to create a single pot. Each pot is a unique blending of the potter's skill and her design vision. Each pot that emerges whole and beautiful from the flames is a gift. Reading the potters' descriptions of their work, I am struck again and again by their sense of the sacredness of the process, the quiet joy they take in creating objects of beauty that once held food and water but now hold their people's history. When I hold a pot, it's as though the potter's own pleasure in its creation is being transmitted through the pot into my hands. It feels good. It feels right. And again, I'm reminded that any work done with joy is itself a beautiful creation.

BY ELLEN PHILLIPS

TWENTY-FOUR

perfection is overrated

As a child, I studied piano with a gray-haired woman who smelled of talcum powder and gave me sugar cookies when I played my scales without mistakes. I was a little frightened of her house—dim and fussy with fringed lampshades, dust-encrusted picture frames, and the gleaming black expanse of her baby grand piano. She corrected me in a stern voice, scowled when I hit a faulty chord, and firmly guided my fingers back to middle C. I took lessons from her for 4 years, then quit because piano didn't come as easily as algebra, poetry, or art—and I didn't want to fail.

Years later, in my 20s, I decided to try again. This time, my piano teacher was an effusive woman who gave me ragtime and jazz tunes along with classical sonatinas and minuets. She had three children, and her house was a jumble of skateboards, jump ropes, and stray mittens; she often had to nudge toys aside to make a path to the piano.

I liked her, but my old habits were hard to flee. I played stiffly, barely tickling the keys, my foot jittery and hesitant on the pedals.

One day my teacher asked, "Why do you play so tentatively?" I remembered my first teacher and her scowls. "I'm afraid of missing a note," I said.

My teacher smiled. "Anndee, the room is full of missed notes." I glanced around at the room's colorful disarray, then back at the piano keys. She was right. I was being too cautious. If I didn't risk missing a note, I'd never play with verve and passion. The reward, this time, would not be a sugar cookie for a perfect performance, but simply the joy of filling the room with music, pure notes and dissonant ones, the expression of a heart let loose from fear.

BY ANNDEE HOCHMAN

TWENTY-FIVE

it's not the size of the gift that counts

In the four years we'd known each other before getting married, not once did my wife's guitar emerge from its dormancy—I'd never even heard her play. The gorgeous 1976 Martin D-35 sat idly by in its case in a corner of the bedroom. It seemed the days of practicing along with records and performing in cafés had fallen victim to the rigors of a budding career and the hustle of city living.

She'd often told me how much she enjoyed playing along with a particular old, rare Neil Young record when she was in college and how she'd wished it would come out on CD so she could hear it again. She was so enamored by this album that she told me she'd researched it and was saddened to read somewhere that a CD release wasn't forthcoming due to some remastering issue or another. I kept this in mind for a few years, occasionally inquiring in record stores and looking on the Internet to see if there was any news on the album's reissue to CD. Eventually, the Neil Young CD did get released, unbeknownst to my wife. When she arrived home from a late night at work, she was surprised to find it hidden under her pillow. I went into the bedroom to find her sitting on the bed, tuning up her Martin and playing along with the CD. She was truly beaming—amazed (*and flattered*) by the time I'd spent researching and looking for it.

My wife and I have always enjoyed giving gifts. We've made it a custom that when we travel, we pick up little things along the way—small, simple, and unexpected things, indigenous to the region we're visiting. Gifting allows us to keep family and friends in our thoughts as we travel and share new experiences with them. After all, gifts, no matter their size, can inspire people. And that's the true joy of gift giving and one of the ways to keep relationships special.

Now the Martin has become a regular guest when we travel to our home in the country for a weekend. My wife sits contentedly on the porch and plays for hours—a true gift for me to see.

BY ROB ULRICH

TWENTY-SIX

take time to stop and taste the chocolate

It's 1961, and a 35-year-old man is reading his newspaper in the Saturday morning prosperity of New Frontier, America, when his sons, eight and nine, come racing into the kitchen. The boys are on a mission. One jumps up and plucks glasses from a cupboard, then slips two spoons from a drawer. The other opens the fridge, emerging with a milk carton, and then a cabinet, which yields a can of chocolate syrup. Moving with the purpose of a surgical team, the brothers start pouring and mixing. Milk sloshes everywhere, high-speed spoons clickety-clacking inside the glasses.

Unnoticed, their father watches them, a naturalist studying chimps in the wild. Before the milk has even stopped spinning, the boys suck it down, in sync and in mere seconds. When they bang their glasses and turn to go back to the Huck-and-Tom adventure they had interrupted for refueling, their father announces his presence.

"Whoa, whoa, wait a minute!" he says. The startled boys stop with the suddenness of cartoon characters.

"Hey, Dad," the older one says sheepishly, instantly aware that they're busted for the mess they've left in their wake, and adds, "Oh, we forgot to put the milk away," as though it was one of those pesky little oversights instead of their trademark.

As they hastily clear the counter, the younger brother wipes up spilt milk with his hand and dries it on his jeans.

"Can I ask you guys something?" Dad says in an inquisitive mood.

"What, Dad?"

"Did you guys even taste that milk?"

"What?" they reply in unison, more confused than two people had ever been.

"You guys drank that milk so fast you barely had time to taste it."

"What?" they said, stumped as to what he was talking about.

"You guzzled that milk down. It was in your bellies before you could even enjoy it."

"Oh, no, we enjoyed it," the older boy said, suddenly realizing that Dad was in his little life-lesson mode and taking the liberty, on behalf of his brother, to assure Dad that, oh yeah, they had really, really enjoyed the milk. Very much. Great milk.

"Oh yeah, we loved the milk," the younger boy added, getting with the program. "It was chocolaty." It was also all over his chin, except for the drop that landed on his sneaker.

"Good. Always remember to taste the chocolate milk," the father said.

This chocolate milk maven, aka my father, had a singular way with gratitude. He took a warmhearted pleasure in the small blessings of the journey. Over the years, his use-your-taste-buds wisdom has come back to me countless times, reminding me to stay in the moment, to notice all the small enchantments along the way. Yes, of course, habit will overcome us as we move through our obligations. And nobody can pay attention all the time—it's exhausting. We actually need a little automatic-pilot time in our lives. But I don't need nearly as much as I usually get. And a long-ago sentence from a father to his sons endures, reminding this grown man that, even through travails, a person can pay attention and savor the chocolaty sweetness of the world.

BY HUGH O'NEILL

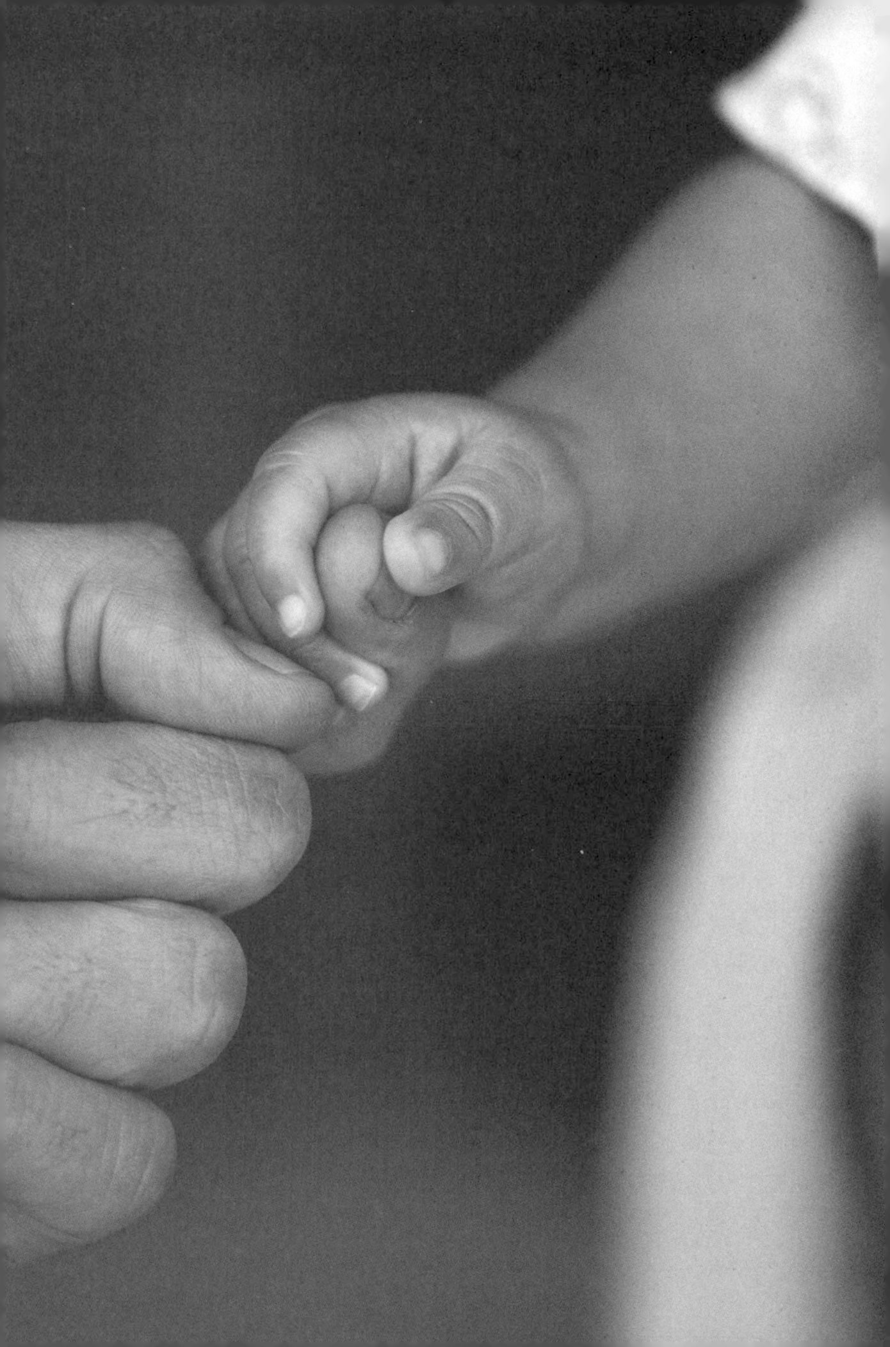

TWENTY-SEVEN

you can handle more than you think

My first child, a girl, was born six weeks early, so Baby Julia ended up spending most of her first month in a "miracle ward" known as an NICU (*neonatal intensive care unit*). Here, modern technology and vigilant staff combine to keep alive the tiniest, most vulnerable new arrivals on the planet—including many babies that only a generation ago would have been literally left for dead.

We would pass these tiny newborns on the way to Julia's incubator. Some weighed less than a pound—lovely little E.T.'s on shiny foil mats, lying quietly in a tank. The babies wore eye masks under bright blue lights (*used to fight jaundice*). At night, the nurses made the room dark, transforming the place into a spooky movie set, the only light emanating from that row of experimental pods containing the miniature masked beings under blue lights.

Julia—all wrinkly and skinny—was among the largest of these kids, but still quite ill. The reflex to breathe is one of the last things to develop in the womb (*since breathing's not necessary there*). So sometimes Julia's body would forget and shut down—setting off alarms until a nurse would calmly touch her back to life, like a wife tapping a napping husband in church.

But the worst came when Julia got a life-threatening infection. One horrible night, I watched as doctors stuck our baby with huge needles for a spinal tap. She was so sick and lifeless, she didn't even stir. But the infection cleared, and weeks later we finally were allowed to strap Julia into a car seat. We drove slowly to our house, placed her on the kitchen counter, and said, "Welcome home."

Upon examining my wife Jenny after Julia's birth, the doctors said the premature delivery was likely a fluke and there was no reason to believe that it would happen again. The doctors lied.

A couple of years later, Jen was pregnant again. Nine weeks before our due date, she began experiencing contractions 2 to 4 minutes apart. In other words, the train was leaving the station. A stay in the hospital put the brakes on for a while (*well, that plus bags full of powerful drugs whose street value no doubt exceeded our enormous hospi-*

tal bill). And then Jen came home.

On the Saturday night after Thanksgiving, moments after I had hung the final string of white lights on my increasingly excessive front-yard Christmas extravaganza, the train began to approach its final destination. After Jen spent weeks fighting a painful, uncomfortable battle against nature and her own body, her water broke. I ran around the house Ricky-Ricardo-style, looking for, I don't know, shoes or a suitcase or something. My mother-in-law rushed over to watch Julia, shrieking that I should bring a blanket and scissors for the frantic 20-minute drive to the hospital.

Scissors?

Less than three hours later, my new daughter Valerie was chillin' in her crib, listening to Sinatra. Well, actually, it was an incubator (*with my tape player propped in there against the glass*). She was small, under five pounds. Many people have no doubt caught fish that were bigger. But we weren't throwing this one back. Valerie's stay in her pod was blessedly less eventful than her sister's. A couple of weeks later, she was on the kitchen counter.

It's been years. Our life now is full of giggles, ballet slippers, basketball practice, and two bright and inquisitive girls. Plus two grateful parents.

There's almost nothing remarkable about this story.

It happens every day. Most families have survived much worse. And to me, that's the most amazing part. Sometimes life does get spooky. But somehow people get through it.

In our case, it was with worry, fear, tears, and prayer. With friends and family and the power of modern medicine. By leapfrogging unsteadily from one doctor's meeting to the next, hour by hour. And by pretending everything was going to be okay.

In the end, for us, it was. The whole experience of the NICU now seems like some dark little forest that we got lost in for a short while. With much help, we were lucky to find a clearing and have rarely looked back. But it's good to know that when the next dark patch comes (*and it will*), like everyone else, we will somehow find a way.

BY NELSON PEÑA

TWENTY-EIGHT

a true surprise is a rare gift

"Why do you always do that?" my wife says, the frustration evident in her voice.

"You told me to guess," I say. "Sorry."

We've had the same conversation many times before. Christmas, birthdays, Valentine's Day, you name the holiday—if there's gift giving involved, there's a good chance I've spoiled the surprise by guessing what her present to me is.

I'm not sure how I developed the skill; reading the look on her face when she says, "You'll never guess this time," remembering conversations about different projects or pastimes when she was particularly paying attention… Honestly, I don't know what it is that lets me confidently say, "A cordless drill" or "The new Allman Brothers CD" or "Those boots I was checking out at REI." But there's a strange pleasure in knowing that I'm right. That I know.

That's why it was so frustrating that, when Jen was pregnant with our first child, she made it clear that she didn't want to know if it was a boy or a girl. How could she not want to know? From toys to clothes to room decorations, I figured that knowing boy vs. girl would just make things easier. Still, I couldn't argue. After all, she was the one carrying the baby, and in my mind, that made her the decision maker.

So I waited, though I often asked, "Are you sure you don't want to know?" The answer was always the same:

"Yes, I'm sure. No, we're not finding out."

When Jen went into labor, I actually didn't think about the boy or girl question. Her labor was tough—labor always is, I've learned—and long. We were in the hospital for over 24 hours before she even started pushing. I'd been there the whole time, of course, but it's not like I could really help. I'm no doctor. All I could do was worry.

Then I saw the head. The anxiety, the waiting, the not knowing of the past nine months came flooding back. And then it was over. The little body came out, inhaled, turned pink, and started to cry. "It's a boy," the doctor proclaimed. Then I started to cry, too.

All the wondering, all the guessing was over in that one spectacular instant. The truth is, my guesses up to that point (*"We're going to have a boy. No, wait. I think it's a girl."*) meant nothing because I really couldn't tell. I just didn't know. And not knowing made the final revelation even more remarkable—as though I was given the chance to make up for all the surprises I'd spoiled over the years. I learned at that moment that true surprise is so rare, so special, that it needs to be embraced at every opportunity.

Now, we're expecting our second child. And when people ask if we're going to find out if it's a boy or a girl, I immediately say no. I don't want to know. I want to be surprised.

BY BRIAN FISKE

TWENTY-NINE

attitude is half the battle

Truth be told, I've never been a great athlete. The sport I enjoyed the most in high school and was the best at—in relation to the other sports I attempted—was cross-country. But even then, I never came close to breaking any records or winning any races. All I could chalk up on my list of accomplishments was completing all the runs—even the long weekend ones we were supposed to do on our own through the "honor system."

In my first actual race, I came in somewhere in the middle, consistent with my usual performance. And considering the hours of training I had put in, I was frustrated.

My coach—who wasn't known for praise, so all his words were worth their weight in gold—pulled me aside at the finish line and said, "You're not real fast and your form could use some work, but I know I'll always be able to count on you to keep on running and do it with a smile on your face. And that's half the battle."

I listened to his "half the battle" feedback with half an ear and then sat under a tree in a semi-sulk. But deep down, somehow his words stuck with me over the years—in my personal relationships, in my profession as a writer, in my still mediocre but diligent running career.

I know and accept that not everyone I meet is going to like me. I know I'm not going to nail every single story I write. And I know I will probably never place in a 5K, much less win one. But sometimes the outcomes of your efforts or the number of people you beat aren't most critical—it's your integrity, the quality of the work you do, and the lessons you learn along the way that really matter.

Just the other day—almost 13 years after that first cross-country race—I was sitting in a job performance review. After getting praised for some things and criticized for others, my boss said, "but when you come in, you check your problems at the door. You genuinely want to do a fine job, you always have a good attitude and, really, that's half the battle."

This time, instead of sulking, I got right back to work. With half the fight won, I couldn't wait to start the other half of the battle.

BY ELIZABETH SHIMER

age is just a number

Every summer in New York State, the small vacation town of Lake George is taken over by families looking to entertain themselves with boating, waterskiing, and a plethora of other activities that call for flip-flops and a bathing suit. But it was also the site of a mission for one 76-year-old woman—my grandma.

She's the kind of woman who buys shoes just because she likes them and worries about what outfit she will wear them with later. She flirts relentlessly with teenage waiters when she goes out to eat. And she's traveled to Europe twice in the past several years. So no one in the family was surprised when she led the way on an afternoon parasailing adventure—it was simply something she'd always wanted to do.

So there she was—strapped into a parachute and sailing high behind a speeding boat, breaking the age barrier people on the shore seemed to place on her with their amazed looks. She was a banner crying out that fun (*even the "extreme" variety*) isn't reserved strictly for teenagers.

Grammy didn't even notice the fuss. She's never gotten locked into "acting her age."

But through the years, she has picked up some valuable wisdom: she ignores the expected and does what she wants. To her, age is just a number (*one that puzzles her but doesn't dictate*). I know 25-year-olds who swap short shirts for business suits, 45-year-olds who exchange a night on the town for too many nights in front of the TV. My grandma wouldn't understand.

Soaring above that lake, she wasn't worried what a 76-year-old should look like. In fact, she wasn't worried about anything. My grandma was simply sharing a bright summer day with her family, savoring the thrill of wind and speed lifting her high into the air. And thanking God for allowing her to fulfill one more dream here on earth.

BY KATIE CHAFIN

THIRTY-ONE

your contribution is more valuable than you might think

He was the most gifted professional I knew. A consummate reporter. A nurturing boss. A caring colleague. It was easy to be in awe of him, and I was.

The problem was, the editor was about to join me, for several days, in coverage of the political campaign I was following. He would be sitting next to me on the press plane, eating the same sterile airline food, reading the same handouts—and watching me write. With that pressure, how could I possibly get through the week?

As luck would have it, it was he who had to write first. He joined the campaign with a notebook full of some Washington development or other and had to write about it aboard the plane, typewriter perched on his knees, before we hit the next campaign stop.

So he rolled the paper into the typewriter, just as I would. He sat motionless for several minutes, just as I would. He typed a bit and rolled the platen up and mulled, just as I would. He xxxxed and mmmmed with ferocity, just as I would. He anguished, just as I would.

And then he did an astonishing thing. He asked me to read, over his shoulder, his raw copy.

Dumbly, I read. He had a word in the second paragraph that was not quite correct. I meekly suggested a replacement. His eyes lit up, and he rolled the copy back down to that spot and inserted my word. My word!

The experience recurred several times before he was finished. And when he had completed the story, he sighed. I looked at him—quizzically, I'm sure. And he said something that, in my naiveté, I thought he had coined at that very moment and realized only years later had been a citation of writer Dorothy Parker: "I hate to write, but I love having written."

It summed up my whole existence. And I loved Max Frankel for having let me see, for the first time in my life, that I was not uniquely insecure. The demigod was merely human.

BY JIM NAUGHTON

THIRTY-TWO

small delights make great discoveries

When my children were very young, we lived down the street from a world-class zoo and would visit it on a weekly basis. Each time the young lady at the entrance would offer us a map showing animals of interest—grizzlies, flamingos, gibbons, otters, elephants, reptiles—a veritable world of variety. And while I embarked toward a different exhibit each time, intending to expose my offspring to the amazing diversity of life, that map didn't begin to cover the wonders my sons discovered.

What fascinated them was not, for example, the widely advertised and much anticipated Komodo Dragon, but, rather, the manhole cover outside its cage. Slightly warped, the heavy metal disc made a deep "clunk" when our stroller wheeled over it. "Mo'!" squealed young Noah, wanting more. So I unbuckled him and watched, amused, as he spent the morning oblivious to the crowds waiting patiently to see a large, lethargic reptile—instead toddling across the loud black circle again and again in a heavy footed trot of delight.

We could, and would, easily spend an hour in the exotic bird sanctuary. Not watching the birds. No, walking through the clear wide plastic strips hanging down in the doorway. And back. And through. And back.

"Peekaboo."

Another favorite spot was the wooded path, home to my son Michael's first favorite creatures. Squirrels. And birds with beautiful black feathers that shimmered with jewel tones—common southern blackbirds with a call as coarse as their names. Grackles.

But the single most memorable discovery was pure happenstance. They found it one steamy August visit following a morning rainstorm. We'd gone with friends and ventured over to watch the usually sedentary hippos swim and snort. Before long, the children noticed something far more interesting. A puddle. A very large puddle. In a flash, one ran through the water.

Wait!" we called. It was too late—all three were soaked before we could stop them.

Back and forth, the children ran. With each step, their

sandals splashed water up to their shoulders, up to their chins. Three children, drenched and thoroughly happy.

We shrugged. "What's the harm?"

This was even more fun than watching squirrels, cackling at grackles, or clinking across a manhole cover.

Our children embraced the wild essence of life with the same abandon as an otter and the laughter of a gibbon. Shedding wet clothing like a molting peacock. Something no caged animal could ever teach them, nor any motherly plan. Instinctively, they celebrated the blessed gift of water on a hot summer day. And, again, taught their mothers to put away the map and cherish all the little moments of delight.

BY JENIFER GENOVESI

THIRTY-THREE

we all have a unique voice...you just have to find yours

My mother was always timid and shy, having grown up with a father and sister who drummed into her head that she was stupid and unattractive, that she had nothing worthwhile to say, and even if she did, she wouldn't know how to say it. So for too many years, she buttoned up.

It didn't help that her husband (*who would become her ex*) was much like her father, reinforcing her fears of lacking anything of note to contribute.

But something happened when my mother turned 50. One day at work, my mother piped up about a movie she'd just watched again, the popular "Close Encounters of the First Kind," or was it "The Wizard of Odd." And something happened when her fellow secretaries heard this. They laughed. Not at her but with her. And it wasn't the last time that would happen.

The waitresses at her neighborhood diner made sure her cup of decapitated coffee was always full because in return they got a laugh. And my mother got a life. She wasn't humiliated, she wasn't humbled—she was human and humorous and in demand! She was playing her own circuit, from the workplace to the auto repair shop, from the dry cleaners to the dinner engagements she now accepted.

Her malapropisms did not diminish, but they no longer defined her in a negative way. They were uniquely hers. Her confidence grew. We all have a voice, she learned, we just have to find it—and embrace it.

BY J.L. GREEN

THIRTY-FOUR

sometimes you've got to think outside the box

Whenever I see a vintage automobile rolling down the road, I'm reminded of the old 1965 Ford Country Squire station wagon my parents held on to long after its prime. Hardly considered a classic, the car sported simulated wood paneling, odd hexagonal-shaped lights, and a general demeanor resembling that of a tugboat. Such a sight on the highways was hardly *en vogue* in the mid-1980s. Yet it ran, and my parents, children of the Great Depression, weren't about to part with something practical, no matter how many stares and giggles it invited from the neighbors.

And so they rose to the challenge when a hole the size of a half dollar in one of the taillights threatened the ability of the car to pass the state's safety inspection. My father, being an engineer, would much rather fix something than buy a replacement. But he needed to get the car repaired immediately so it could pass inspection and be driven legally. Begrudgingly, he set out to buy a new taillight.

"You want what?!!" was the flip response from the dealership. "We haven't stocked that part for over 15 years, buddy." After enduring that jeering, my father called a number of junkyards trying to locate his elusive taillight. He finally found a place that had an exact match, but the owner, obviously sensing he had the most holy grail of car parts, was asking an exorbitant price for the bounty. Dad refused to give in to such an outrageous demand. I wondered what he would do.

One evening, I was welcomed home by a foul, unidentifiable stench emitting from the kitchen. I noticed my father hunched over a pot on the stove, cooking some sort of red paste. Then I saw the ransacked rolls of cherry-flavored Lifesavers lying on the counter. I followed him outside and watched as he painted the red, sticky goo in the hole with a Popsicle stick.

"Won't it melt, Dad?" I asked.

"As long as nobody runs up and licks this light, we should be in good shape," he replied.

Who was I to argue? He was the engineer in the house.

I wondered how my dad reasoned that cherry Lifesavers would solve the problem. It turns out that my mother had shown him a recipe for "stained-glass cookies," in which you could make "stained glass" from colored Lifesavers.

Well, the car passed the inspection, and that taillight remained unblemished (*and unlicked*) for years, saving us the expense of a new car.

BY ROB ULRICH

THIRTY-FIVE

35

family goes beyond blood

Holiday dinners, birthdays, graduations, quiet times of just being together…I come from a large, close-knit family. So when I married a military man and moved a thousand miles from home the day after our wedding, many people warned me that I was in for a whopping case of homesickness and loneliness.

They were right—but not in the way I had expected. I was lonely. I was desperately craving the comfort (*and the comfortableness*) of my family. But most of all, I simply longed for people who knew who I was, who I had been, and who I had the potential to be. It caught me off guard, this keenly acute sense of being misplaced and forgotten. Sure, we knew many people, but everyone was in constant motion. In the military, I missed the feeling of permanence.

Then one night, something happened. One of my

new friends showed up on our doorstep after a house fire, with nothing but her infant son and the clothes on her back. (*She wasn't even wearing shoes.*) While her husband salvaged what he could from their home, we made tea and dug through boxes of old baby clothes.

Once everyone was settled for the night, I had the chance to sit down and take in everything that had just happened. I thought about how under different circumstances the woman in my guest room would have gone to her family, but instead she came to me. She chose our home because she knew she would be safe and accepted. We did not share a single gene, but we did share ourselves. On that night a new family was born. This new family blossomed slowly, not like the instant and seismic love of a parent for a child, but a gentle and shy recognition of shared ideas and mutual respect…the recognition of my own feelings reflected back at me from another soul.

That one night with her allowed me to open myself to the families-in-waiting that had been there all along. The neighbors who brought me dinner after we moved into a new house; the woman who took my child to school when I had the flu; the friends who let me just be me. All of the quiet, simple things that I treasured so much in my family were found in the people that I had chosen to be my friends.

It has been years since that night, but the lesson is one I cherish: She chose us to be her family, and in that instant, we were.

BY AIMEE LANGAN

THIRTY-SIX

it pays to approach new things with an open mind

When I was 36, my doctor recommended that I get my first mammogram. As a writer specializing in health-related topics, I'm a big fan of regular screenings, so I nodded vigorously and scheduled one right away. I can't say I particularly looked forward to it, but I didn't dread it either. It was a rite of passage. A fact of life. Something I would be proud to say I had done—if only to encourage others to do the same.

When female friends and family would ask what's new, my upcoming mammogram was on the list of things I'd mention—along with my new hip-hop dance class and my recent passion for scrapbooking. Then the horror stories started flooding in, including a particularly disturbing meant-to-be-funny E-mail poem about the pain, pressure, and personal humiliation associated with a mammogram.

As I lay in bed the night before my test, I wondered if I should be more anxious about the whole thing. Would it really be as bad as other women said? Would it be worse? Then I had a flashback to when I was pregnant with my first child and was similarly inundated with lurid tales of epidurals-gone-wrong and excruciating back labor. I'm happy to say that although my daughter's birth wasn't as pleasant as downing a carton of Ben & Jerry's, it wasn't as awful as some births…nor as easy as others. But it was uniquely my own and undeniably worth every twinge. My mammogram experience, I told myself, would be the same.

Having sufficiently calmed myself, I decided to try to be open-minded and work with my technician to have the best experience possible. And I think I did. The technician was pleasant and kind. The facility was clean and offered free coffee. I was kidless for the hour, so I even got to read a magazine in peace for a few minutes. And after the mammogram was over, I treated myself by purchasing a delicate handmade butterfly pin from the gift shop downstairs.

The mammogram itself wasn't great. It wasn't awful. But the experience was uniquely my own and undeniably worth every twinge.

Now if only I can approach my next high school reunion with the same positive attitude.

BY LAURA QUAGLIO

THIRTY-SEVEN

you can't always go it alone

Abandoned railroad tracks led up the mountainside to the remote village of Peguche, Ecuador. I followed them past two llamas, past two old women herding goats, past a waterfall. Finally, I came to the little whitewashed, tile-roofed hostel called Aya Huma that I remembered well from my earlier travels with a friend. I had returned this time to live alone for several months and write a novel.

I chose a room with white walls and bright striped curtains. My windows looked out on chickens in a garden of roses and calla lilies. The volcano loomed off to one side with its patchwork of corn and bean fields climbing impossibly steep slopes. For 10,000 sucres a night ($4 U.S. dollars) I had this room and a private bath with a hot shower to myself. I could not believe my good fortune.

Along with farming, the indigenous people wove wool sweaters and blankets to sell in the marketplace; their thumping looms the heartbeat of the village. In the evening, men played Andean panpipe music in the hostel's little cafe where I took my meals. The wood-raftered dining room would be crowded then, full of life. But mostly my days in that magical place were spent in solitary pursuit. With only a few months to write a manuscript, I kept myself to a rigid schedule. I had no phone, no friends. I was going it alone, no matter how lonely I felt.

One Sunday morning, while the village slept, I sat at the hostel's near-empty café and poured blackberry syrup on my banana pancakes. My young waitress approached me with a letter postmarked from Holland. She told me in Spanish that the old Andean woman in the corner needed the letter translated to her in Quechua.

"But I don't speak either Dutch or Quechua," I told the girl.

"That's okay," she said. "You're the missing link."

Besides the waitress, the old woman, and me, the one other person in the café that Sunday morning, amazingly, spoke only Dutch and English. What were the chances of this?

We arranged ourselves around a table. The Dutch woman translated the letter to me in English. I, who spoke only English and Spanish, translated the letter to the young waitress, who spoke only Spanish and Quechua. She translated to the little old woman, who spoke just Quechua. Only through the combination of us four could an understanding be reached.

The letter was notification from the Dutch government that the Andean woman's son must appear for a court date in Holland if he wanted his car back. The Andean woman waved her hand at us and grinned a gap-toothed smile. "Oh," she said (*her words translated back among us*). "Is that all? He's lost two cars already. What does he want with that one?"

I had thought, at first, that the letter would carry some special significance or news. But it turned out that the written words weren't what mattered. The letter delivered to me a greater truth: sometimes you can't go it alone.

BY CHRISTINE SCHULTZ

THIRTY-EIGHT

the most meaningful legacies can't be measured

For as long as I could remember, my grandmother Lucy did not work outside the home. Though I'm told she held paying jobs until shortly after I was born, the woman I remember was a housewife, grandmother, crafter, and unparalleled cook, especially around the holidays. Growing up, there were typical Italian Christmas Eves—including seafood and zeppoles—and Easter bread in the spring. There were handmade holiday ornaments throughout my childhood and bridal dolls and baby blankets as I made my journeys into married life and motherhood.

My grandmother was the one I called for help when I was newly married and attempting to make my first Thanksgiving turkey. As she offered her comfort and consultation through the phone, cradled between my shoulder and ear, I—donned in rubber gloves and some serious self-doubt—held the turkey in the kitchen sink. Soon we were laughing so hard that I was crying at my ineptitude over merely washing this bird. But I got through it—with just a little bit of help from Lucy.

But the greatest lesson she taught me was to enjoy life to its fullest. And that's what she did.

On my grandmother's last morning alive, I thanked her for all that she had done for me and let her know that it was okay to leave this world. I found a hairbrush in her bedside table and brushed her hair, remembering how I had done so as a child and how she had washed my firstborn daughter's hair after I brought her home from the hospital.

I thought of the old adage that says that when death is on your doorstep, you're probably not wishing you had spent more time at the office and you're not hoping someone reads your resume at your funeral. I'm positive that in her few remaining moments, Lucy was not wishing for either of these. This was a woman whose legacy was not a multimillion-dollar corporation, but rather a loving family and a well-lived life.

Once while visiting her in the assisted living facility where she spent her last few years, I noticed a message board in the hallway that read, "I've learned…that the best classroom in the world is at the feet of an elderly person." I count myself lucky to have been one of my grandmother's students.

BY CHRISTINE A. KRAHLING

THIRTY-NINE

meaningful is more beautiful

For years, I was a beauty junkie. I moved to towns known for their physical loveliness—Boulder, Colorado, San Francisco—believing the splendor would seep into my bones. By living in a beautiful place, I would live a beautiful life.

To a certain extent, the magnificence did make life easier: it's hard to wake up and look at the morning sun dancing on the Flatirons or the Golden Gate Bridge and think you have it too tough. I felt like I was on vacation every day. I'd take the 10 California bus to Ocean Beach, past the riot of hibiscus bushes, and stroll down a path lined with eucalyptus trees grinning like a fool. Planting my bottom on the warm sand, I'd stare up at the undulating green of the Marin Headlands and wonder, "How did I get so lucky?"

Still, more often than not, I found myself looking around for someone to share it with, someone with whom I could trade grins and say, "Are you getting this? Can you believe it?"

I had plenty of new friends, but they'd all been raised in these mountains and valleys. They relaxed into the beauty with the nonchalance of bored teenagers watching TV in their parents' den. They teased me for my rhapsodic swooning. It was, after all, their birthright.

For a while, I struggled with the "if only's"—if only my family were from here, if only they'd settled in the Bay Area instead of Bayonne. I'd come back East for the holidays, bundling against the harsh damp chill, and try to convert other colonizers. "Come out West with me," I said. "You won't believe how dazzling it is."

But none of my childhood friends would even consider leaving the East Coast. Family was here. That might be a nice place to visit, but this is home.

Then I got married, and my husband's need to be with his family trumped my addiction to Pacific sunsets. We moved back home; I cried the day I handed in my California driver's license. San Francisco showed up in my dreams like a beloved friend who'd passed away too soon. Strip malls and gridlock had replaced wild roses and golden sunsets. I was inconsolable.

A few months later, after many interminable Sunday dinners and petty sibling spats, I was sitting at my sister's kitchen table, half listening to her tell me about a new Crock-Pot recipe while I watched my niece dismantle her dad's carefully constructed jigsaw puzzle. I shared a wink with my mom, and we both bit our lips to keep from ratting her out. The door burst open, and my husband and brother-in-law stomped in carrying stacks of wood, letting in a shock of winter air. The fire stoked, my niece climbed into my lap, clutching a book I'd read to her 10 times that morning. As her tiny body wriggled to get comfortable, I felt a slow buzzing warmth rise up in my chest. In an instant, I saw very clearly that my life had become indescribably richer because I had stopped rambling around those lonely tourist spots. Some things are better than sunsets.

BY MARISKA VAN AALST

just sitting can be pure joy

There is a list on my desk, a page ruffled on one edge where I tore it from a spiral notebook I keep in the car. At the top it reads: walnuts, tuna, eggs, butter, baby carrots. Below that: go to bank, file bills, bring clothes to homeless shelter, make dinner date with Mom. On the side, in tinier printing because I was running out of room, I jotted down our menus for the next three nights.

That's just one list. There's a separate agenda for work, with deadline items in boldface. There's a list of house repairs—Patch bedroom ceiling! Get estimate for stonework pointing!—with exclamation points to underscore urgency.

I relish checking items off my lists, tangible marks of accomplishment and industry. And I've always been like this. Whether by nature or nurture, I got the habit from my mother, herself an obsessive list maker who still works full-time, keeps a social calendar that makes me look like a recluse, and routinely accomplishes more in a day than many people do in a week.

Four years ago, when my daughter was born, I raced off to the hospital with lists in hand: relatives to call after the birth, questions to ask the pediatrician. And then I brought my daughter home—five pounds and thirteen ounces of undiluted, 24-hour-a-day need.

Suddenly, I couldn't make lists because my left hand was always busy: cradling a baby, maneuvering her in and out of the bathtub, functioning as an ever-ready pacifier, pinky finger plugged into her rosebud mouth. Even with a hands-free telephone headset and a sling carrier, I was unable to multitask. In my sleep-deprived state, I had to focus 100 percent in order to do anything on the precipitous learning curve that is early parenting: change a diaper, warm a bottle, find just the right syncopated back pat to soothe Sasha's cries. Whole days slipped by, and I floated with them, untethered by agendas.

One bright Sunday I decided to take Sasha to an art museum an hour away. As soon as we arrived, she began to sob with hunger. Flustered, I plopped down on a bench in the first gallery, several rooms away from the drawings I'd come to see. Sasha ate. I sat. And because there was nothing else to do, I looked at the paintings, a collection of large portraits. I noticed the way honey-colored light bathed the face of the young girl in one painting, the stiff-shouldered bravado of a boy's pose in another, the deeply lined cheeks of an old woman in a third. The more I looked, the more I saw. Shadow and expression, a gnarled hand, a sideways glance.

By the time Sasha finished, the museum was almost ready to close. I breezed quickly past the drawings, then packed her into the car. As I drove home, my mind, for once, didn't jump ahead to the next day's plans. Instead, I focused on each pure and present moment: russet leaves waving against a Wedgwood sky, the hint of cider from a roadside stand, the steady rhythm of the car rocking us home.

BY ANNDEE HOCHMAN

FORTY-ONE

it's up to you how colorful your life is

Many years ago an interior decorator told my mother that the most elegant color for any home was white. Taking the words to heart, she and my dad bought gallons of "candlelight" colored paint and rolled any color out of the series of homes that we lived in. My mother took comfort in a decorating style that incorporated her fondness for white-on-white fabrics and glass-top tables. It was safe and easy.

My mother had a safety plan for her young charges as well. My sister and I were encouraged to stay inside and romp around a family room filled with dozens of oversized white pillows. This way, there was little chance that we would track in dirt across our pristine carpets. And inside, there was no possibility that we would fall out of a tree or off a bicycle or merely trip on the sidewalk.

The plan worked. While other kids at school were able to proudly show off the traditional rites of youth: bruised knees, arms in slings, and the ultimate multi-colored badge of courage—the autographed plaster cast, my limbs (*just like the carpet*) remained mar-free.

Soon I found myself voluntarily adopting my mother's "safe" ways from the clothes that I wore (*"White goes with everything," my mother had taught me*) to the ginger ale I drank by the liter (*less likely to leave a stain if spilled*). My vacations were spent at home reading about places I had never been, activities I had never attempted.

Then everything changed. I met a man who would encourage me to wear red and tell me with genuine affection how good it looked on me. With him, I developed a taste for new types of foods, sports, and outdoor adventure. He became my husband.

Now what to most would seem like ordinary experiences, to me has become a brand-new world. I've climbed a mountain to witness the migration of hawks and view spectacular fall foliage. I've stood among a thousand screaming teenagers at a Britney Spears concert as an avalanche of yellow confetti fell from the rafters. I've clung nervously to my husband while cruising along the narrow roads of Bermuda on a moped (*as he ironically belted out "Born to Be Wild"*).

With every new experience, I still feel like a child—thrilled by the newness of it all, searching with my eyes, trying to take it all in, and wanting to touch everything.

Not every adventure has been a stunning success (*I need never ride a horse again*), but my fear of roads less traveled has lessened. After all, walls can be repainted, cherry water ice stains can be washed out of clothing, and bruises left by a galloping horse will heal.

BY SUZANNE CHANDLER

FORTY-TWO

even the wounded have the capacity to heal others

Four months after our 14-year-old daughter Kate was hit by a car and nearly killed, we had to return to the hospital for some follow-up surgery. It was a triumphal return of sorts because by all accounts she never should have survived the accident. But not only did she survive, her recuperation had been nothing short of miraculous, and her prognosis was good.

The day after the surgery, when she was understandably woozy and recuperating in the pediatric ICU, a funny thing happened. One by one, totally independent of one another, the medical staff who had treated her came to her bedside, each saying essentially the same thing. "Kate, you wouldn't remember me," they'd tell her (*and of course she wouldn't; she was still barely conscious at the end of her stay there*), "but I worked with you when you were here this summer. It's good to see you." Nurses, doctors, therapists, clergy, social workers, even volunteers joined the queue until, after about a dozen or so had come by, I pulled one of them aside.

"Nancy, it's wonderful that you've all taken the time to come by—it means a great deal to us," I told the nurse, "but I get the sense there's something more going on here than meets the eye. I get the sense you folks need to do this."

"We do," she told me. "You see, for every ten kids who come to us as seriously injured as she was, there's maybe one Kate, one kid who beats the odds and makes it through." She told me that they needed to see her because it's that joy that sustains them through all the pain and sadness they see the rest of the time. "It's what keeps us coming back and doing our job."

I think of that extraordinary staff as having served Kate—and us—through the most difficult days of our lives. I think of them as healers and as portals of hope. It never occurred to me that this was a two-way street. Here was Kate, healing them, giving them reason to hope, and showing them that in final analysis we are not alone; we all have the capacity to sustain one another through our shadowed valleys.

BY ERIC KOLBELL

FORTY-THREE

love is bigger than squabbles

Throughout the years, the dynamics of my family seemed sort of like plate tectonics. Sure, we'd all start from the same place, have the same origins, but different groups of us would split and drift away. Instead of seas and mountains separating family members, gulfs of silence and walls of stubbornness would divide us. And like many other families, such strife ran through generations.

The first time I'd realized there were such divisions was in my late teen years. As a child visiting relatives in Kentucky, one of my favorite stops was my Aunt Louise's house. I spent several summers there in my pre- and early teens helping her tend her garden and playing basketball with my cousin. Somewhere during that time, my mother and aunt stopped talking to each other over some now-forgotten dispute. When on vacation, we didn't visit my aunt, and if I ever questioned my mother, she'd brush it off, usually with a headshake and silence.

Once my brother and sister and I had graduated college and began our own little continents, my mother's personal tides moved her back to Kentucky. She renewed friendships and started a new life there. Yet, despite living just a few country miles from my aunt and passing her regularly in town, she still didn't speak to my aunt. The silence roared like waves for years.

Then came the diagnosis: My mother had advanced lung cancer. And the prognosis was poor.

She was proud and wanted to bear it herself, only telling a few people close to her. But it was a small town, and soon my aunt found out. Once Louise heard, she opened her house to my mother. My aunt went with my mother to treatments, helped by grilling doctors, and the two became close again. After a bad turn, my aunt set up a room in her house with a hospital bed and even assisted my mother in bathing and getting dressed. Throughout the final days of the illness, my mother and aunt reconnected, rehashed stories about growing up on a farm, and talked about their hopes for their children. When my mother died, my aunt was there, right beside her.

During the days surrounding the funeral, I, too, became reacquainted with my aunt and introduced her to my children. She'd tell my kids embarrassing stories about me growing up, and we both flipped through picture books to catch up on too many years lost. Now my children and I regularly visit my aunt. There are calls, cards, and a connection that wasn't there before, but was simply waiting to be rediscovered.

Whenever a loved one dies, we seek out some purpose, some reason for why things happened. With my mother, it was clear: To reunite a world that had been divided.

BY DOUG DONALDSON

FORTY-FOUR

you can be anything you imagine

I was a shy kid but became a fairly confident adult—at least, by all appearances. Meeting people, especially in the workplace, was still a nerve-racking experience for me. I imagined that everyone else knew what they were doing and was doing it well, and I was the only one unsure and unsteady.

Then, one day while heading into the office, I timidly greeted the guard at the entry to the building. And he smiled back. Emboldened, the next day I said hello to the guard again, and then even gave a nod to the guy down the hall, who responded in kind. I bumped into a colleague at a luncheon soon after and smiled from across the room, approached with a firm handshake, and received the same in return. Before long, I was displaying a new sense of confidence among my co-workers and, ultimately, my formerly intimidating boss.

Sure, I had to fake it to make it, to really feel capable, but it worked for me. If I could have looked at things logically instead of emotionally, it would have been clear that I was doing fine on my job and had nothing to be afraid or ashamed of. But I was psyching myself out with my doubts. So I pretended to be confident—my own version of method acting.

It worked so well that I was invited to speak at an industry convention. Heading there, I happened to be on the same train platform as someone I'd met just a short time before, a former sales manager who had done countless presentations. He gave me this advice: They don't know what you're planning to say, so they won't know if you make a mistake. If you miss something in your talking points, relax and keep going. Well, I stood before the crowd and made my speech. And when it was over, knocking knees gave way to hobnobbing handshakes and congrats and requests for more information. I was one of them! In fact, I was now guiding them.

I had overcome my doubts and took an internal bow for a good performance.

BY J.L. GREEN

FORTY-FIVE

the world is filled with wonder

My eleven-year-old daughter is still losing her teeth.

"Guess what, Dad!"

"Well, let's see...are you getting married?"

"No," she giggles.

Then she shows me that she's placing yet another enamel chunk, a proxy for a future credit card purchase, under her pillow. "So, what's the Tooth Fairy going to bring me this time?" she asks.

"How about Bill Gates for a new dad?"

My daughter's last tooth earned her a ruby and diamond encrusted gold Rolex watch-well, not really, it was from the Wal-Mart Signature Collection at 50% off—but on my income, it was a splurge.

Still, I'm not complaining.

I remember when I was a kid, a thousand and fifty years ago; I awoke one Saturday morning to find a much-longed-for baseball mitt hanging on my bedpost. It was the same glove I'd been dreaming of, the one I'd been pleading for, promising never to ask for anything ever, ever again if only my parents would buy it for me.

But my parent's had repeatedly told me NO—that's right, in loud capital letters—because they said they couldn't afford it.

And yet, when I found it magically hanging there, courtesy of the Tooth Fairy—or so they told me—it turned that Saturday into the happiest and most memorable day of my young, innocent life.

My 11-year-old daughter, though, says she doesn't believe in the Tooth Fairy, Santa Claus, leprechauns, or little elves. She says she's too old to believe in fairy tales. But I know better. She does. We all do. We have to. Our dreams, fantasies, and wild musings are our pots of gold at the end of reality's rainbow.

Sure, my daughter knows that the Tooth Fairy is just me playing a game, hiding a gift under a pillow. But she also knows, way deep down, that under her pillow, behind closed eyes, is a winsome, mystical place of good and kind thoughts. It's where she keeps her never-to-be-lost wonderment and innocence—the same wonderment and innocence we all keep and cling to. Some of us may hold to it secretly, some overtly, and some just need to be reminded how and where to find it again.

Whenever I suspect I've lost that sense of wonder, I think of a child's gleaming smile and tight squeezing hug. It's in a giggle, a kiss, a dollar found on the sidewalk. It's in a butterfly fluttering delicately across a green lawn. It's in a ladybug crawling on your finger. It's in a warm handshake, a heartfelt thank-you, an unreturnable favor. It's in a misty morning sunrise and a spreading fire sunset. It's in the pleasure of giving. It's in a seed sprouting into a flower. And it's in a Wal-Mart watch found under a pillow where a tooth was placed the night before.

BY BARRY DENSA

NO
COMMERCIAL
TRAFFIC

FORTY-SIX

sometimes the cynics are just plain wrong

This wasn't how it was supposed to end. My laughing kids rushing around the Thanksgiving table to jump onto my lap and hug me. Warmth. Love. Joy. A momentary glimpse of perfection in a world spinning too fast.

No, it was supposed to be different. This day was supposed to be a disaster. At least according to almost anybody I mentioned it to. In fact, when I said I was planning to drive to New York City for the Thanksgiving Day parade, the standard response was sometimes stated, sometimes implied, but almost always the same:

"What? Are you nuts?"

The plan was simple (*at least to me*). Drive into Manhattan with my wife and kids the night before, stay in a hotel, get up early to grab a good spot on the parade route, eat our Thanksgiving meal at a wonderful restaurant, drive home.

They tried to warn me. Traffic would be hell. The hotel would be overpriced and dingy. Parking would be impossible. The crowds would be overbearing. And, oh yeah, it's late November in New York. You're going to freeze.

As Thanksgiving approached, I almost started to believe them. I thought about canceling the whole thing, but the hotel seemed solidly non-refundable. I was stuck.

So we went. Driving into the city that Wednesday afternoon, we did see a ton of traffic (*heading the other direction*). Our reasonably priced, low-hassle hotel was a comfy, friendly oasis—with valet parking and a doorman who helped unpack the family van.

On Thanksgiving morning, I got up early and walked the couple of blocks to the parade route, carrying blankets and hoping for a front-row spot right on the curb. My wife and kids stayed at the hotel getting ready, waiting for my cell phone call to find out where to meet me. It was three hours before the parade, but I couldn't find a front-row spot until I noticed an opening behind a newsstand—a place everybody seemed to be ignoring—and spread my blankets.

Before long, a rumor spread. The woman next to me said the reason these spots were open was because we were too close to the end of the parade route. She said the parade goes completely silent on this block to keep sound from interfering with the national TV broadcast at a reviewing stand just a few blocks away. A moment later, she was gone, having gathered up her blankets and walked uptown, where she didn't expect to find a front-row spot; but at least she'd be sure to hear the bands and feel the drums. I almost followed her, but decided to take a chance and stay.

Waiting for the parade to start over the next couple of hours, it did get crowded. But nobody seemed to mind. I hung out with families from Mississippi, New Jersey, and Brooklyn. Every time members of the N.Y.P.D. would stroll down the parade route, we cheered. The bigger hams on the force responded with mock parade-style waves or a tip of the hat.

My wife and kids arrived, and the parade started. The crowd surged, but we were shielded by the newsstand behind us. Blind luck. We leaned back and the newsstand became own personal reviewing stand.

I'm not a guy who especially likes parades, but this one blew me away. My kids got to pet the passing horses and high-five the clowns. During a lull, my daughters even held one of the guide wires of the legendary big balloons. The bands boomed. (*That rumor had been wrong. The silent mode started on the next block.*) The temperature was in the mid-60s. Nobody froze.

At the restaurant, we still had confetti in our hair. It was the most stress-free Thanksgiving meal ever (*no turkey to worry about, no plates to scrub*). And when it was over, spontaneously, the kids hugged their daddy.

Miss out on this just because something might go wrong? What? Are you nuts?

BY NELSON PEÑA

FORTY-SEVEN

we can surmount tragedy with love

As an ordained minister, I'm always honored to be asked to bring my craft to the service of an old friend. So it was a pleasure to accept the invitation of my college pal Peter to perform his wedding to Siobahn.

In sitting down to talk about it, we knew that it was going to be a stylish, elaborate, spare-no-expense affair; Peter lived large and did so unabashedly. What we didn't know was that two weeks prior to the wedding date terrorists would fly commercial airplanes into the sides of our city's two tallest buildings, killing, among others, friends and colleagues.

As I sat in my office in those stunned days following the attacks, I thought about the wedding and about what a pointed contrast it posed: the extravagant celebration in the wake of the unspeakable tragedy. I had a very difficult time crafting the ceremony. Words didn't come. Creativity was not in the air. I knew that we could not use an occasion such as this to dwell upon the horrors of September 11, nor could we charge ahead as though blissfully ignorant of them.

So I called the couple and asked that we meet for dinner. Perhaps something would come of it for me. Something did. At one point during the meal, I turned to Siobahn and said, "You have put an enormous amount of time and money and energy into this affair. You've paid such close attention to seeing to it that it all happens just as you've envisioned it. But in light of what has happened, how have things changed? How are you feeling about it all now?" She gave me a perfect answer.

"Now," she said, a winsome smile crossing her face, "it really doesn't matter what color the napkins are."

No it didn't. For all of the opulence and attention to detail that once defined this wedding, the focus had shifted. For the better. Because now what mattered was that we would all be there, all be together. Family and friends would gather and again reaffirm that human beings are capable of surmounting great tragedy with even greater love. Everything else—the flowers, the food, the music, even the color-coordinated napkins—would serve as mere window dressing (*granted, elegant window dressing*) to this one undeniable truth.

BY ERIK KOLBELL

FORTY-EIGHT

you can live richly, and money has nothing to do with it

Forty sketches were due at the end of the week. As I put my things together, I lingered over my sketchbook. The cover was bright blue and spiral-bound; the pages were thick, blank, and full of possibility.

It was midterms at the American University Center of Provence, where I was studying abroad for my junior year in college. In lieu of classes, we had a day to study. Outside my host family's home, I pulled the gate closed and felt especially relaxed as I set out on my usual route to school. Every day, I passed the same fruit and vegetable vendor, where I would sometimes stop in for a tomato or an apple and practice my grocery vocabulary. I passed the same café with the floor-to-ceiling windows where I would see the same old men sidled up to the bar with their little espressos and morning cigarettes.

With the 40 sketches in the back of my mind, I noticed a wrought-iron gate that gave entrance through a cement wall I had always taken for granted on the other side of the street. Feeling like I had some stolen time, I wandered across the street. The gate was unlocked and led to stairs that immediately descended into an artfully designed courtyard. Sidewalks divided the park into equal parts and joined to form a circle around the fountain in the center. The park was part of an art museum, which looked like it was just closing for the lunch hour. I set up shop on a bench facing the fountain. As the sun warmed my face, I took off my jacket and remembered reading in a travel book that you should always dress in layers during the fall in the south of France. I took my sketchbook out of my bag and assessed potential subjects. One child raced giddily around the fountain, another dangled her hand to test the water, and a couple was picnicking in a sunny corner.

Opening my book to a fresh page, I faced the fountain and started to outline the curves of the structure. I heard my painting teacher's reminder in my head, "Forget the intellect." She repeated the phrase so often it was more of a mantra. They were Cezanne's words, meaning: don't think about drawing something. Be open to your impression of the moment.

Birds brought movement to my page. I made lines

until they took form, would flip without resignation to a new start, and shift position to a new composition. Deep lines. Splashing water. Fountain. Children. Birds. I remember looking up and feeling my good fortune and taking note. I wasn't in it for the grades. I didn't need to be anywhere. I didn't want for anything. I was just living—calmly, graciously.

I had wanted so badly to extend my stay in Aix-en-Provence, but there was no way. By the last week of the semester, I was literally living on soup and bread, and I traveled home without a dime. But I took that day, that moment in the park, with me. That moment—of wanting nothing—is my most cherished possession.

BY RACHEL MARUSAK

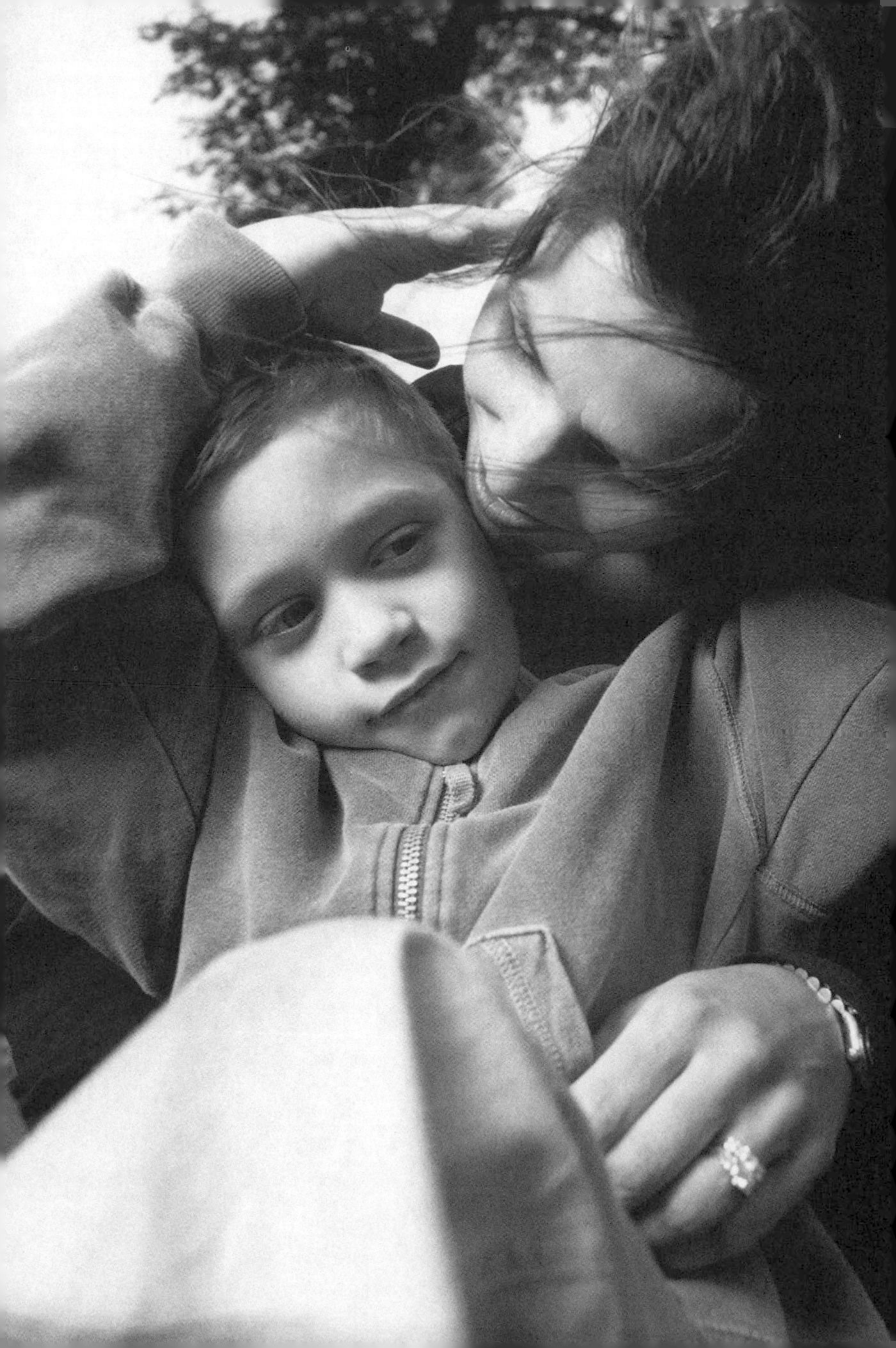

FORTY-NINE

on your to-do list, it's a good idea to put people first

I once had a friend who said she wanted to give her kids her "undevoted attention." At the time, I thought it was a funny slip of the tongue (*I knew she meant undivided attention*), but for some reason her words stuck in my mind...only to return to haunt me about a week ago.

It was not an unusual day—just a bit busier than normal. I was faced with the inevitable list of to-dos—planning a scouting meeting, chaperoning my son's field trip, shuttling my daughter to and from an after-school activity, and getting homework done and checked. I have learned, over the past seven years of parenting, to juggle such things pretty well (*most of the time*). But I've also found that adding one extra to-do to my list (*in this case, the field trip*) can be fatal. It threw off the delicate balance of my life, which left me careening from one activity to another instead of calmly striding through my day.

At 4:30, I was frantically zipping my kids into their coats when—in a surprising moment of clarity—I realized that I had not heard a word my daughter said since she got off the bus. And my old friend's words bubbled up from the depths of my memory. Undevoted attention. That was exactly what my kids had been getting that day. Although I had been doing things for them every minute since I'd awakened, I was too frenzied to so much as exchange pleasantries. And didn't they really deserve better? For that matter, didn't I?

And so I stopped. I stopped cramming my daughter into her coat. I took a deep breath. And I looked deep into her eyes, apologized, and asked her to tell me (*again*) about her day. When she'd finished, I hugged her, found my son, and asked him to do the same. It took all of 10 minutes. We were 5 minutes late for my daughter's dance class. And I was the happiest I'd been all day.

BY LAURA QUAGLIO

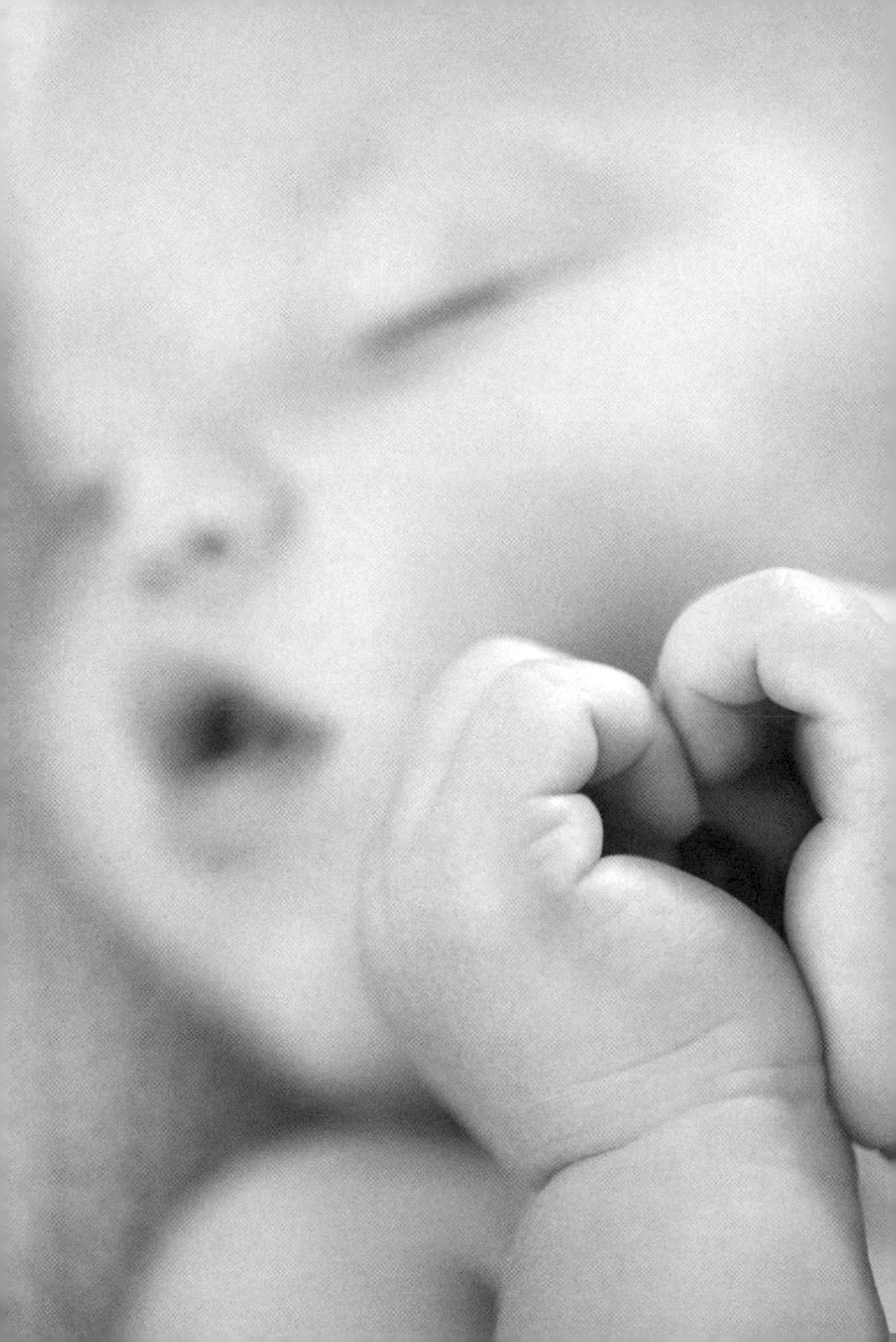

sometimes it's what you don't ask for that is the very thing you need most

The festive feelings were gone from Christmas that year in my parents' house north of Boston. Only the trappings remained—the food, the tree, the presents. Once the gifts were unwrapped, we could think of nothing to say to each other. We escaped to separate rooms—Dad to his basement computer, my sister to the TV upstairs, my older brother out the door to a friend's, me to the kitchen. The house seemed as silent as snow. Then I overheard my younger brother Tom talking to my mother in the living room.

"Mom," he said, "you're going to be a grandmother."

"Oh, no," she said.

Tom was 22 then, with two years left of college. Kim had been his girlfriend only three months. My mother wanted to be happy for him, but wasn't.

I moved to the doorway. Within a few minutes, the others came, too. We hadn't truly communicated in so many years that now we struggled to do it. Tom said he wanted to do the right thing—get married, raise a family, find a job. His studies could wait.

I was worried he would waste his mind for invention. "Remember those wild contraptions you used to make," I said, "how you always wanted to be an engineer."

My sister cried. (*She never cries.*) "You're my baby brother," she said.

"I know you think it's the right thing now," said my father, "but give it more thought. I got married two weeks after college, had you four kids within the next few years. If I had it to do again, I'd do it differently.

When you're young, there's so much open to you. I missed out on it. Don't you."

Tom listened to what we said, though I'm not sure what he thought. We weren't a family used to giving advice.

The following summer, on August 17, Zack was born—eight pounds seven ounces, with brown eyes that jolted like coffee beans. He was no longer just a worry, he was real.

That Christmas, no one drifted to separate rooms. We stayed to watch Zack smile and gurgle and reach out to draw us near.

As he grew, he learned to please: reciting Dr. Seuss

stories by heart before he could read; singing "Little Jack Horner" to laughing applause; exclaiming over shirts and socks as if they were gifts a four-year-old boy wanted most in the world. He brought Christmas to our house again. All dimples and brown eyes, his voice filled with pleasure, he said, "Isn't this great? Isn't this just great?" Because of him, it was.

Because of Zack, Tom ended up staying in school so he could get a good job in robotics. He and Kim turned out to make a terrific match. They married and had a daughter who became great friends with her brother Zack.

After all these years, it's easy to forget that Zack was once the boy whom none of us wanted. The boy who had worried our family—and who, in so doing, made us realize we still were one.

BY CHRISTINE SCHULTZ

If you have enjoyed this book or have your own Truth Worth Knowing that you'd like to see in future books, we would love to hear from you.

Write us at:
Book Feedback
Mail Drop 215
2501 McGee
P.O. BOX 419580
Kansas City, MO 64141-6580

or E-mail us at:
booknotes@hallmark.com